D0596526

TO

_____

FROM

_____

DATE

_____

Huddle Up! 40 Sports Devotions for Coaches and Parents of Teen Athletes
Copyright © 2018 by Mark Gilroy Creative, LLC
www.markgilroy.com
First Edition, March 2018

Published by:

DaySpring

P.O. Box 1010
Siloam Springs, AR 72761
dayspring.com

Written by Mark Gilroy
Cover Design by Gearbox (studiogearbox.com)

Printed in China

Prime: 71921

ISBN: 978-1-68408-212-4

HUDDLE UP

40 sports devotions for coaches and parents of **TEEN** athletes

MARK GILROY

FOREWORD BY MIKE MATHENY
Manager of the St. Louis
Cardinals and
Best-Selling Author

"I love it when coaches look at sports as a way to mentor young athletes in character development, which is the real reason we play the game. *Huddle Up!* is a great resource to help both adult supporters and youth participants keep their focus on what matters most, becoming exceptional men and women of faith, character, and values."

– Tommy Kyle,
Executive Director
of Nations of Coaches

"For many of us, playing sports was our most passionate endeavor as we grew up. I absolutely love how *Huddle Up!* weaves lessons on faith, life, and sports to help young people keep their eyes on the real prize—loving and serving Jesus Christ."

– Collin Klein,
Heisman Trophy finalist
and Quarterback Coach,
Kansas State University

CONTENTS

THE RIGHT TEAM

FOREWORD

My Christian faith has been the guiding principle of my life as a player and manager. I'm so grateful for parents and coaches who have encouraged me in my personal walk of faith. That's why I am so delighted to endorse *Huddle Up!*

When our children huddle up with God, they learn so many important lessons in life: faith, teamwork, preparation, resilience, discipline, how to handle defeat and success, goal-setting, trusting others, hard work, and the simple pleasure of doing one's best.

If you are a parent reading this, the greatest encouragement you can give your young athlete is the "strong, silent support" that shows you trust that God has put your child with the right coach and the right team at the right time. No game or season will be perfect, but give your son or daughter the space they need to learn the lessons that God has prepared for them. Most of all support your child and their coach with prayer.

If you are a coach reading this, thank you for your commitment to providing a fun, positive, skill- and character-building experience for our young people. Like me, I'm sure you can think back to the coaches and other adults who helped you grow up and grow stronger in your faith. You have a great opportunity to be that same kind of influence to a young person this season. Compete hard, teach hard, but most of all, pray hard for the children God has entrusted to you.

When we huddle up as parents, coaches, and young athletes, we come together to reaffirm our strategies, our plans, our goals, and most of all our belief that God knows us, loves us, and has wonderful plans for our lives.

That's always the right team!

– **Mike Matheny**
Manager, St. Louis Cardinals and author of NY Times best-selling book *The Matheny Manifesto*

INTRODUCTION

Time to *HUDDLE UP!*

We love sports because not only are they a lot of fun, but they remind of us some of the most important life lessons: commitment, discipline, handling adversity, teamwork, focus, poise, and so much more.

Since you love sports too, *Huddle Up!* is written to show you the impact of the Bible in every area and activity of your life.

Huddle Up! shares real insights and questions from peers to help you enter into a short but hard-hitting look at God's Word. Each Bible study ends with a great opportunity for you to apply God's Word to your own life and to make a personal commitment to living for God. Take the time to turn the "Game Plan" suggestions into action.

Are you ready to grow closer to God?

Then it's time to *Huddle Up!* and make your spiritual life a priority!

HOW TO USE THIS BOOK

Fun Ways to *HUDDLE UP!*

Huddle Up! is a great resource to guide you in your personal devotions. Real-life sports scenarios will grab your attention and help you discover just how relevant God's Word is for every area of life—including your favorite sport!

Huddle Up! is perfect for your coach or team sponsor to use before or after practice or on a road trip with your entire team. The devotions are life-related, and the activities will help you and your teammates weave your faith into the sport you love so much.

Huddle Up! works great for family devotions. You and your parents can discuss ways to give your best in sports—but, more importantly, in your faith. Families that pray together grow stronger together!

Huddle Up! can be used by you to lead a Bible study with a few of your friends. Sports instill discipline and leadership habits that will last a lifetime. God's Word instills values that stay with us throughout eternity. This is an excellent way to pass on what you are learning with your peers.

What's the best way for YOU to Huddle

TRAIN HARD

For physical training is of some value,
but godliness has value for all things,
holding promise for both the present life
and the life to come.
I TIMOTHY 4:8 NIV

I'm going into my junior year of high school football. I played JV last year and have a chance of starting on Varsity this year. This summer I've been hitting the weight room every morning at six before I go to work. A lot of my good friends think I am crazy. I'm so tired at the end of the day that I have to hit the sack early. My friends laugh at me for not hanging out late. Even my mom thinks I am working too hard.

I am beginning to wonder if I'm putting too much effort into football.

—John, age 17

There's an old saying that says, "Whatever you do, do it to your best of your ability." It is inspired by a Bible verse that tells us: "And whatever you do, whether in word or deed, do it all in the name of the Lord Jesus, giving thanks to God the Father through him" (Colossians 3:17 NIV). But here's the deal. The Bible verse wasn't talking about every single activity we do. It was directed to areas of our lives where we can choose either to be resentful or choose to be a positive witness.

Doing absolutely everything to the best of our ability is a good thought but probably not realistic. Not everything we do is of equal importance. Not everything we do matters as much to us. Not everything we do is a demonstration of our faith and integrity. It is no sin or lack of commitment to be casual about many of the activities in your life.

But if being the best you can be on the football field and as a teammate is a big deal to you, make it a big deal in your off-season training. Don't do as little as you can; do all that you can. Put in extra time in the weight room and on the track. Go the extra mile. Your determination, sacrifice, and work ethic will be a witness to your friends and teammates. And, by the way, it will increase your opportunity to be a starter and make your team better.

The apostle Paul has been described as a small man. We know from his church letters that he had some physical limitations, including poor eyesight. He was probably not an athlete, and if he was alive today, he wouldn't be on the football team or basketball squad. But Paul paid attention to sports and admired the commitment athletes made through their training. When he wrote a letter to Timothy, a young man that Paul "coached up" to be a mighty man of God, he used the athlete's training regimen as an example of what matters most: "For physical training is of some value, but godliness has value for all things, holding promise for both the present life and the life to come" (I Timothy 4:8 NIV).

So how much work do you put into your sport? How hard should you train? Godliness must come first in life. But your commitment to off-season training has tremendous value. We all know natural athletes who don't put in the training time and hurt themselves and their teams when it's game time. We also know overachievers, friends who aren't necessarily the best athletes but who work so hard that they outperform more gifted athletes and inspire teammates to do better.

Going to bed early and getting up early to hit the weight room is a great witness to being the best you can be. The discipline and sacrifice will spill over into other areas of your life. Your hard training will prepare you to make tough decisions in the future, even when the right decision is the hard decision. Most of all, your hard training will be a wonderful reminder that godliness requires good decisions and sacrifice.

TRAINING TIP

You can't win a championship in the off-season, but you can lose a championship in the off-season by not training hard or getting yourself ready to compete at your best level.

GAME PLAN

Evaluate how you train. Are you setting yourself up for success? Have you made off-season training a priority? Do your training habits reflect the value you place on your sport?

Now write down some training goals and get started!

PRAYER

Heavenly Father, help me to pursue godliness with the most passion in life. I am committed to living for You and being a witness of the difference You make in my life.

TOUGH TIMES

God is our protection and our strength.
He always helps in times of trouble.
PSALM 46:1

I've been doing gymnastics for as long
as I can remember. I have pictures of
me tumbling on the mat when I was only
three or four years old. I'm ranked in my
region of the country and was hoping to
place in Nationals this year. My coach and
parents thought I have a good chance.
The problem is, my knee started aching a
month ago. I just found out I have a torn
meniscus. That means no Nationals, which
will hurt my chances of getting a college
scholarship. I am so bummed. After all
the work I've put in, life doesn't feel very
fair right now.

—Mindy, age 16

One of the greatest heroes of faith is the apostle Paul. Churches, hospitals, schools, and even cities are named after him to honor his great contributions to the Church of Jesus Christ.

He wrote thirteen letters in the New Testament, and almost half of the book of Acts (chapters 9 and 13–28) is written about his life.

You would think that a man who was that successful in building God's kingdom would have probably had everything go his way. But that is not even close to the case. He had an incredibly tough life.

These are just a few of the really terrible things that happened to him—

- He was shipwrecked (Acts 27:13—28:10).
- He was imprisoned for preaching the gospel (Acts 16:23).
- He was criticized by church people who liked other leaders better (II Corinthians 10:10, 12:11).
- He had physical problems (Galatians 4:13).
- He was stoned by a mob and left for dead outside the city (Acts 14:19–20).

Despite all these incredible difficulties, Paul was joyful (Philippians 2:29)—and he trusted God to take care of him and make him a conqueror in all of life's situations (Philippians 4:13). Paul was living proof that it's not what happens to us but how we respond to our circumstances that matters most.

When God's people were going through a particularly tough time in their history, He sent a prophet to remind them: "Don't be afraid, because I have saved you. I have called you by name, and you are mine. When you pass through the waters, I will be with you. When you cross rivers, you will not drown.

When you walk through fire, you will not be burned, nor will the flames hurt you" (Isaiah 43:1-2).

Hard times are inevitable, particularly if you are a committed athlete. Injuries, tough losses, and other disappointments are inescapable. But whatever the situation, when life gets tough, don't give up or lose faith. Trust God! Your best days are still ahead of you.

TRAINING TIP

As hard as it is to be sidelined from a sport you love because of an injury, it is much better for your future in sports and in life to make sure you are healed up before vaulting back into competition. You have one job right now: Get better.

GAME PLAN

Just because you are sidelined doesn't mean you have nothing to do. A physical therapy program to recover from an injury can be slow and boring. It is often done without your teammates around. Make it a point to be the best patient you can possibly be. Consider it an investment in your future performance.

Are you doing all you should be to recover from your injury?

PRAYER

Dear God, help me to trust You when times are tough. Help me to know You are doing a special work inside of me even when I go through trials.

JUST LOVE

All people will know that you are my followers if you love each other.
JOHN 13:35

My favorite sport has always been soccer. Last year I finally grew a couple of inches and put on some weight. I've gotten stronger and faster. My game has gotten much better. I got invited to play for a higher-ranked travel team and said yes. I'm playing better than ever, but now it's not as much fun. At first, I thought the guys didn't like me, but after being on the team for a while, I finally figured out that no one likes each other very much. I'm used to being best friends with my teammates. It's really hard to be on a team with everyone fighting and putting each other down.

—Jay, age 14

What you are experiencing is nothing new or unusual. We live in a fallen world, and people have been fighting ever since Adam and Eve were booted from the Garden of Eden (Genesis 3). Conflict can even happen among Christians. When Peter wrote to a small group of Christians who were persecuted and made fun of for being followers of Christ, he said: "Always be ready to answer everyone who asks you to explain about the hope you have" (I Peter 3:15).

That means that all of us should be prepared to tell others how we know God is real and has made us into a new person through Jesus Christ.

Have you ever thought through what you would say to someone who wants to have a personal relationship with God? Do you have a couple of Bible verses memorized that you could share with them? Would you be ready to pray with them?

But just as important as having words to say is the way we live our lives. Many people have quit going to church or attending a Christian youth group— or quit a team—because of the lousy attitudes of the group members or because of how badly they are treated.

Jesus tells His followers that the easiest way people will know we have a real and powerful relationship with God is by how we love one another.

One of the greatest and most powerful expressions of love is found in I Corinthians 13, where Paul says: "Love is patient and kind. Love is not jealous, it does not brag, and it is not proud. Love is not rude, is not selfish, and does not get upset with others. Love does not count up wrongs that have been done" (vv. 4–5).

You are on a team where there is little or no love among teammates. Can you fix it? Maybe or maybe not. But you can do your part to change how people get along with each other through your attitudes, actions, and words. Are you willing to show love to your teammates even though no one else is trying very hard?

Sometimes all it takes is one person to make a huge change in a family, a church, a youth group, and, yes, even a sports team!

Are you willing to take the first step? Are you willing to be a leader? It just might make your team a much better experience for you!

TRAINING TIP

Great teams are not primarily motivated to beat other teams, but to win for each other. Love is always stronger than hate. Whether you are playing with a band of brothers or sisters, make sure you have your teammates' backs!

GAME PLAN

Read through I Corinthians 13:4–7 again. Then answer the following questions in how you relate to your team members:

Are you patient?
Are you kind?
Are you rude?
Do you hold grudges?
Are you irritable?
Are you resentful?
Even if you are the only one trying to build a bond, are there some areas where you can grow?

PRAYER

God of love, help me to show the love You have put in my heart by how I treat others. Help me to share love in my family, in my church, and with my coaches and teammates.

FORGIVE ANYWAY

Christ accepted you, so you should accept each other, which will bring glory to God.
ROMANS 15:7

I'm just an okay golfer. I play on Junior Varsity at my high school. I'll be a junior next year, so that will be my last real chance to make Varsity. This summer I was playing in a local golf tournament along with a few of my friends from the high school team. I was doing better than usual and was in the final round, and I had a chance to finish in the top three. One of the younger girls who plays on Varsity was in my foursome. She hit a drive in the rough. I don't think she saw me, but I saw her pick up the ball and move it to a better lie. I was shocked. I couldn't believe she cheated. I let it distract me and my game fell apart. She ended up taking third place. I'm still furious with her.

—Carrie, age 16

How quick are you to ask for forgiveness and forgive others? Nothing will make your soul smaller than to refuse to ask for or grant forgiveness.

Forgiveness is that wonderful expression of love that God shows us through how He treats us and commands us to practice so we don't all destroy each other!

There are a number of reasons we struggle to truly forgive others:

Fairness

It's true, forgiveness isn't fair. But if we all got only what we deserve, none of us would have a chance to be at peace with God and others. God wasn't fair with us as sinners—He was merciful (Romans 5:8).

Pride

We also struggle to forgive because of our pride. If we "let someone off the hook," we wonder how we can feel good about ourselves and whether others will just take advantage of us. God wants you to love and respect yourself, but He also wants you to show mercy to others like He has with you.

Pain

Some people have hurt us deeply—and really aren't looking for forgiveness. This makes forgiveness extremely difficult and painful. In some cases, forgiving others doesn't guarantee that you will have a good relationship with that person—or should even be around them. But even if forgiveness doesn't change that person—it does change you for the better in your heart.

It is important to note that forgiveness doesn't mean we allow others to cheat us or that we don't confront someone who is doing wrong. If you tell an opponent or teammate that you saw them cheating, you give them an opportunity to do the right thing and make it right. If they refuse to and lie about it, that's their problem, not yours. But don't carry a grudge in your heart. Take the matter to God and let Him work inside of you.

TRAINING TIP

The world would be a much better place if everyone sought and extended forgiveness. But we know that is often not the case. What is your responsibility? You are responsible for what is in your heart. Be ready to ask for or extend forgiveness!

GAME PLAN

Is there someone special in your life who has hurt you? Are you still harboring bitterness? Have you withheld forgiveness? Write down what you would like to say to that person. Putting it on paper can help you clarify your thoughts.

Now ask God to restore your love for that person and ask Him to give you an opportunity to talk with them.

PRAYER

Dear heavenly Father, thank You for the forgiveness You continually offer me. Please heal my heart as I choose to forgive those who have hurt me today.

REMEMBER TO REMEMBER

8

Let us, then, feel very sure that we can come before God's throne where there is grace. There we can receive mercy and grace to help us when we need it.

HEBREWS 4:16

The best thing in my life right now is playing travel basketball. It gets me away from my homelife. My parents fight all the time. Everyone used to get along pretty good. Then my dad lost his job. He is working again, but he doesn't make nearly as much money as he used to. He drinks a lot more too. Now all I hear about is how many money problems we have. My mom says we may lose our house. I honestly don't care about the house. I want my family back. When I talk to my coach, he tells me he is praying for me. That encourages me, but I still feel helpless about my situation.

—Jeremiah, age 16

When we get to the end of our own strength, when there seems to be nothing we can do to change our situations, it's good to remember:

- God sent a rainbow to Noah as a symbol that His love for man would never waver (Genesis 9:14–15).

- God spoke to Moses in a burning bush (Exodus 3:2–6) and parted the waters of the sea with His breath to free His chosen people from captivity (Exodus 14:21).

- God allowed a young shepherd boy to conquer a mighty warrior with only a slingshot and a single stone (I Samuel 17:49).

- Jesus healed a blind man (Mark 8:22–25), a person with leprosy (Matthew 8:2–3), a man who had never walked (Matthew 9:2–7), and even raised a young girl from death to life (Luke 8:51–55).

- The Holy Spirit came upon the followers of Jesus so they could proclaim God's love in languages they'd never spoken (Acts 2:4–8).

Why do these long-ago things matter? How do they help us today?

One of the key words in the Bible is "remember." We are to remember God's mighty works, His mercy, His faithfulness, His kindness. Sometimes we forget all God has done for us, which only makes our current difficulties harder.

Remembering that God is at work in our world—and in your life—is what gives us the hope that if we hang in there and keep the faith, our best days are yet to come. He has been faithful for countless others who are in need—and He will be faithful to us!

Sometimes all we need to do is open our eyes and see that God is near and ready to help us. Sometimes we have to have patience. His answer to our prayers may take time because He is working in the hearts of others. But don't give up. Be bold as you go to God in prayer.

Keep your eyes open. Look around. You might just see a miracle today.

TRAINING TIP

In the heat of battle, when it's fourth quarter in a close basketball game, it's easy to lose our poise and make costly mistakes. Sometimes that happens not because we aren't trying hard, but rather because we are trying too hard and trying to force something to happen. When the pressure is on, it's even more important to remember our training and stick to the plan.

GAME PLAN

Find some time to write down the gracious deeds the Lord has done for you since you've been walking with Him. Tuck your list into your Bible and look at it from time to time.

As you remember what God has done for you, be bold and encourage others with your testimony.

PRAYER

Dear heavenly Father, thank You that being Your child means seeing Your comfort and provision in every detail of my life. Thank You for Your goodness.

THE CHOICE IS YOURS

You have begun to live the new life, in which you are being made new and are becoming like the One who made you This new life brings you the true knowledge of God.
COLOSSIANS 3:10

Nothing seems to be going right in my life now. I've never been a great student, but my grades are so bad that my wrestling coach told me I may not be eligible to compete the rest of my season. I have to go meet with the school counselor to find out if there's anything I can do to squeeze by. I'm not sure how I got so far behind on everything. I've always had a big problem with procrastinating. I make a promise to myself that I'm going to change and get ahead on things, but then I fall back into the same old pattern of waiting until the last moment. I'm not sure I have the ability to change.

—Anthony, age 14

For centuries, people have debated what makes a person who they are—are we born the way we are, or do we become the way we are through the things that happen to us?

Some psychologists believe that everything a person does is determined by the shaping influences in their lives, like parents and life experiences—and some go so far as to say that once a person is five, their personality is shaped and can't really be changed.

Other people think that we are primarily a product of genetics, that our behavior and attitudes follow from the way we are "wired." Common expressions of this idea would include: "I can't help it; it's just the way I was born"; or "A leopard can't change his spots"; or "The nut doesn't fall far from the tree."

The answer, of course, is both. We inherit some of our attributes through our genes, and we pick up some attributes through our environment. But don't forget that the biggest influence is our ability to make good choices. The power of personal choice is a gift from God to each of us.

The biggest choice we will make is how to response to God's love. When we do, miraculous changes become possible. When we say yes to God, He is able to change even the most stubborn, damaged, sinful heart.

Paul makes this point clear when he writes to us, "If anyone belongs to Christ, there is a new creation. The old things have gone; everything is made new!" (II Corinthians 5:17). After changing our hearts when we are saved, God isn't finished with us either. Paul says: "We all show the Lord's glory, and we are being changed to be like him" (II Corinthians 3:18).

But you don't understand how I've been brought up. You don't know the mistakes I've made. You don't understand how hard it is for me to stop doing some things you might say.

With grace, with faith, with the help of godly friends, you can say along with Paul: "Forgetting the past and straining toward what is ahead, I keep trying to reach the goal and get the prize for which God called me through Christ to the life above" (Philippians 3:13–14). Because of His forgiving, life-changing power, God's ultimate concern with your life is not where you've been, but where you are going.

Can you change? When you say yes to God, you will receive the ability to make all kinds of changes, big and small.

TRAINING TIP

Good coaches, supportive friends, and good training habits are proof that you have the ability to improve, grow, change, and become better. Think of how far you've come in your sport. Realize that God is ready to do the same thing in all areas of your life.

GAME PLAN

Identify a new attitude or a new habit you want to develop in your life. Or identify an old attitude or habit you want eliminated from your life. Commit this change of heart to God and ask Him to do a special work in you. You might experience an instantaneous, miraculous change—or you might experience a gradual growth and change.

Either way, don't forget that God is the Source of your strength.

PRAYER

Thank You, O God, for making me a new person through Your Son, Jesus. I ask You to continue and complete the good work You started in me.

DETERMINATION

I do not mean that I am already as God wants me to be. I have not yet reached that goal, but I continue trying to reach it and to make it mine.
PHILIPPIANS 3:12

I'm in my final season of high school soccer. I'm probably not good enough to play in college, but I've had a blast. At least I was having a blast, until the start of this season. Our coach got pregnant and had to give up the team for the season. I think the new coach must have been a drill sergeant for the marines. I've always been ready to work hard, but his practices seem ridiculous. I actually thought about quitting. Something interesting happened, though. We started winning more than we ever have. I'm having my best season ever. I always thought we were in great shape, but the new coach has taken us to a higher level of conditioning and playing. I am so glad I hung in there!

—Jennifer, age 18

Philippians is known as a book of joy. Some form of the word "joy" appears in nine verses in this relatively short letter, despite being written by Paul from a Roman prison. In both his words and his actions, Paul encourages us to be glad in spite of suffering (chapter 1), in the midst of humble service (chapter 2), and in the face of fear and anxiety (chapter 4).

But is it practical to think that we can rejoice in any and every situation? When a parent leaves? When a friendship crumbles? When a family member hurts us? When a teacher or coach is particularly hard on us?

Note that Paul does not say to be happy because of hardship; he says to rejoice despite and in the midst of pain. Paul doesn't call us to wish for hardship and pain in our lives, but he does call us to be overcomers in all circumstances.

James says much the same thing when he tells persecuted believers: "My friends, be glad, even if you have a lot of trouble. You know that you learn to endure by having your faith tested. But you must learn to endure everything, so that you will be completely mature and not lacking in anything" (James 1:2–4 CEV).

Paul knows what he's talking about. This is the man who was stoned and beaten (Acts 14:19, 21:30–32), shipwrecked (Acts 27:39), suffered from a painful physical sickness (Galatians 4:13–14), lived with the guilt of being a persecutor of innocent people in his past (Acts 22:4), and was imprisoned and sentenced to death for his faith (Acts 16:22–24). But like the Energizer Bunny, he just kept on going and going and going.

Why? How? He was a man of joy.

Paul's final message to the Philippians concerns

the way this church cared for him during his trials. He says that their gifts and compassion were "a sweet-smelling sacrifice offered to God, who accepts that sacrifice and is pleased with it" (Philippians 4:18). Helping someone else persevere is a fragrant, pleasing prayer to God! Do you have a teammate who needs encouragement?

Yes, life can be difficult. But even in the midst of suffering we can stand firm—and help others to do the same—as we joyfully keep going with God's help.

Now, the challenges we face in sports are not the same as outside persecution or tragedies. In sports, we volunteer, signing up to exercise discipline and perseverance through hard training. That's one of the things that makes your sport so valuable to your life. It teaches you the rewards of endurance for other areas of your life, including your faith.

The good news is that perseverance and failure cannot coexist. Why? Failure only happens when you quit. That's a great reminder to keep going!

TRAINING TIP

The Navy Seals have a principle called the 40 Percent Rule. Simply stated, when your brain tells you you're wiped out and can't do any more, you're actually only 40 percent done. So keep going!

GAME PLAN

If life is more like a marathon than a sprint, why not walk or run your own personal spiritual "marathon" today? No, you don't have to cover twenty-six miles on foot, but plot out a nice, long course, start walking, and spend the time talking to God about the various challenges you are facing now, thanking Him for His help in each step of your journey ahead and praising Him that He loves you and cares about all areas of your life.

Through prayer, God is your partner, no matter trail you are on.

PRAYER

Thank You, heavenly Father, that no matter what challenges I face today and tomorrow, You provide me with the physical, emotional, and spiritual resources that I need.

GOD CAN USE YOU

8

But Moses said to the LORD, "Please, Lord, I have never been a skilled speaker. Even now, after talking to you, I cannot speak well. I speak slowly and can't find the best words."
EXODUS 4:10

My coach told me to relax and enjoy myself. My teammates have been very encouraging. But I'm worried sick. I've never pitched before and tomorrow afternoon I'm starting. We've had a bunch of injuries this year, and our top two pitchers are out for at least a couple of weeks. We're in a tournament, so Coach said they need me to make a switch the first game. I've played outfield my whole career. I'm absolutely willing to do anything to help the team win, but I'm afraid that using me as a pitcher will guarantee at least one loss.

—Abby, age 14

We live in a competitive, dog-eat-dog world. As an athlete, you already know how hard it can be to go against elite competition. But it's not just sports. We can turn ourselves inside out with worry, because sometimes it seems like only the smartest, the most athletic, the best looking, and the most near perfect have a chance to succeed.

Many of us question our abilities and are fearful about testing our wings and attempting all that God has called us to do.

If you ever struggle with healthy self-confidence, note that one of the greatest leaders in all of history, Moses, had the same worries and doubts. When God called him to lead the children of Israel out of Egyptian bondage, Moses was full of excuses.

He let God know he couldn't do it.

They won't listen to me. I stutter. Send my brother. I just want to be a simple shepherd.

Maybe it was the trauma of separation from his parents as a baby and being adopted into a "foreign" culture. Maybe it was the guilt of things he'd done in his youth or being raised as a prince while his own family served as slaves. Whatever the reasons, Moses had deep fears about whether he was good enough to do what God wanted him to do.

But God was patient with Moses. When he finally trusted God and stepped out in faith to confront the pharaoh and help forge a free nation, he took to heart God's promise to him: "I will help you speak, and I will teach you what to say" (Exodus 4:12).

Yes, we should continually improve ourselves. It's good to strive for excellence in our lives. But we can't forget that God often gives us things to accomplish that are beyond our abilities. But because of His help, He can use us no matter what seems to stand in the way.

No matter how much "work" you think you need right now, be assured that God can use you just as you are.

TRAINING TIP

Know what you're good at in sports—and life—but don't be afraid to step outside your comfort zone. A willingness to try new workouts, new positions, and new sports will make you more versatile and improve what you are already good at!

GAME PLAN

What is one thing you want to accomplish that you've never started? Who is one person you want to meet but have never spoken to? What is one thing you feel God nudging you to do but have been afraid to try?

Determine one step you can take forward and prayerfully go for it this week!

PRAYER

Lord, thank You that You use us to do big things in the world. Help me to hear Your voice and do all that You've called me to do.

YOUR FUTURE HOPE

"I say this because I know what I am planning for you," says the LORD. "I have good plans for you, not plans to hurt you. I will give you hope and a good future."
JEREMIAH 29:11

I can't believe it is already here. The last game of my entire football career is less than a week away. I've had plenty of bruises and aches and pains, but I've loved every minute of being a football player. I know it sounds mushy, but I really do love my coach and the guys on my team. A lot of us have been playing together since the fourth grade! I'm not sure I'll be playing in college. I have a couple of offers from some small colleges. But whether I play or don't play at the next level, I'm feeling sad about losing this team. I'm also nervous about the future. I'm just hoping I meet friends like I have now.

—Stephen, age 18

Jeremiah is known as the "weeping prophet" because he cried so much. He felt such grief for his people. Imagine losing absolutely everything you hold dear—family, home, country, church, even friends.

Jeremiah was devastated by what had happened to his people. King Nebuchadnezzar of Babylon had conquered the kingdom of Judah, destroying the walls of Jerusalem and the temple built by Solomon. The strongest and most educated youth were led off as captives to serve the conquering king. They left behind the city they loved in smoldering ruins.

This young man of God preached to the Hebrew exiles, who now lived in the foreign country of Babylon, along the banks of the Tigris River. The Israelites had lost all hope. How could they think of themselves as God's chosen people under such circumstances? They were slaves, after all.

But even in the middle of all hopelessness, this young prophet, Jeremiah, called to speak for God at an early age, dried his eyes and boldly proclaimed a new promise—that God had a future filled with hope for these people. God had not forgotten His people. That promise did come true for the Hebrew children, and the promise still echoes and holds true for God's people today.

You may feel comfortable about the future—or you may be anxious about all the decisions you face and where they might take you. What's next for you? College? Jumping right into a job? How will your friendships change? Will you live at home for a period of time, or will you move out right away?

No matter what your situation, the truth is that God created you for His glory (Isaiah 43:7) and given you special gifts to make a difference in the world.

Just as He had a plan for His people thousands of years ago, He has a plan for you—a good, pleasing, and perfect plan. And He is trustworthy to make that plan happen, no matter where you are on the journey.

TRAINING TIP

You've heard the phrase, "Your future begins today." Our ultimate future hope is secured by God's promises to us and His love for us. We have the hope of eternal life. But God calls for us to make choices today that impact our future. In athletics, it's easy to observe the results of lifting weights and other training habits to improve our performance. We get bigger and stronger. The same principle is true in all of life. What choices will you make today that will create a better future for you spiritually?

GAME PLAN

In a journal or on a blank sheet of paper, write a list of nine things you would love to be a part of your future. Number each of them, one through nine, and then write down the number 10. Next to that number, write, "Whatever God wants for me."

Commit your whole list to God but pray number 10 the most—"God, I'll do whatever You want me to do."

PRAYER

I do not know what is next in my life, but God, I trust in Your love and Your promises, and believe in my heart that a bright future awaits me.

YOUR TRUE MEASURE

In Christ we are set free by the blood of his death, and so we have forgiveness of sins. How rich is God's grace, which he has given to us so fully and freely.

EPHESIANS 1:7-8

I'm on the 4 x 100 relay team for my high school track team. We were having a great season until our district meet. We had a pretty good chance of making State. I was running the third leg. Everything was so smooth in prelims. But in the finals, I dropped the baton on our handoff. It was one of the worst feelings I've ever had. I let down my friends and cost us a chance at State. There were a lot of tears for all four of us but right now, I feel so bad about myself that I'm numb. I don't know how to face the people who were counting on me.

—Angelique, age 17

One of the great temptations of our day is to believe that we are lovable on the basis of our performance. If we do everything right, then people should love us. If we mess up, we are unlovable.

No wonder we find it so hard to share our true selves with others. We put on masks. We pretend to be what we aren't. Deep down, a lot of us are afraid that if someone were to truly know us—really get to know the core of our being—then there is no possible way they could love and respect us.

The amazing truth of our Bible study passage is that God, who knows us best, also loves us the very most. The verbs found in Ephesians 1 wonderfully describe God's love for us and are powerful expressions of the intensity of His feelings for us: He chooses us; He lavishes grace on us; and even before we were born, His plan was for us to be His children.

We also read in this chapter that He redeems us and forgives our sins through the sacrifice of Jesus Christ.

What makes this love even more remarkable is how happy it makes God to meet our needs. He loves us "according to His good pleasure" (v. 9 NKJV). It pleases God to love us. Just as a parent loves her child, so God loves us (v. 5).

But how well does God really know me? Does He really understand how bad and ugly my attitudes and actions have been? Does He know all the mistakes I've made? Be assured, God knows everything—and He lavishes His love on you with full wisdom and understanding (v. 8).

If the two great needs of being human are to love and to be loved, then you are doubly blessed because of God's love for you. That gives you all the reasons and resources you need to love others—and yourself.

TRAINING TIP

It is right and good for you want to do your very best; to perform well in sports and in life; to be successful. But your true value as a person is not measured by an applause meter; it is measured in the heart and mind of God.

GAME PLAN

On a piece of paper, write out Psalm 139:13–14: "You made my whole being; you formed me in my mother's body. I praise you because you made me in an amazing and wonderful way." Tape it to your mirror and say a prayer of thanks every time you read it.

But don't stop there. If you're not feeling so great about yourself, one great way to lift your spirits is to help someone else with the same struggle. Write a note to a friend with the same scripture passage and a list of things you like and admire about that person.

All of us feel insecure from time to time. Be an encourager!

PRAYER

As my Creator, You knew me before I was even born. You know everything about me—my weaknesses as well as my strengths. Thank You for loving me as I am, dear God.

A NEW MIND

For as he thinks in his heart, so is he.
PROVERBS 23:7 NKJV

I have a bad habit that I can't seem to control. I've become a Christian and go to church now. I pray every day. But I can't stop using bad language. Real bad language. Thoughts and words that I don't want to have just pop out. I'm not the only one on my lacrosse team that uses bad language. And one of my friends says that it doesn't matter how we talk. God doesn't care if we cuss and swear. I just know for me it matters. I want my thoughts and words to be different than they used to be. I could sure use some help with my thought life.

—Zach, age 16

STUDY VERSES: Ephesians 5:15–20

It's tough to keep a pure mind in our culture. We're constantly slammed with images and words that go against what we know is good and right. Renewing our minds is a tough battle, but it's absolutely necessary. Once we lose control of our thoughts, we often lose control of our behavior.

So how do you keep a clean mind in dirty world? You will see a huge difference in the way you think by:

- Committing yourself to God: "So brothers and sisters, since God has shown us great mercy, I beg you to offer your lives as a living sacrifice to him. Your offering must be only for God and pleasing to him, which is the spiritual way for you to worship. Do not be shaped by this world; instead, be changed within by a new way of thinking. Then you will be able to decide what God wants for you; you will know what is good and pleasing to him and what is perfect" (Romans 12:1–2).

  When you declare that God comes first in your life, your mind-set begins to change because of the power of God working inside you. You immediately are less selfish. You're not as comfortable with certain kinds of negative and profane thoughts, either.

- Getting rid of negative messages: "But now also put these things out of your life: anger, bad temper, doing or saying things to hurt others, and using evil words when you talk" (Colossians 3:8).

  Garbage in, garbage out. Whatever we feed our mind is what ends up working itself out in our spirit and behavior. Just as Joseph fled from temptation (Genesis 39:12), so you must flee from certain negative images and words.

- Filling your mind with good thoughts: "Brothers and sisters, think about the things that are good and worthy of praise" (Philippians 4:8).

  It's tough not to think about certain things when you're trying not to think about them! The key is to replace bad thoughts with good ones. Start filling your mind with positive images and thoughts.

- Being filled with the Spirit: "Do not be drunk with wine, which will ruin you, but be filled with the Spirit. Speak to each other with psalms, hymns, and spiritual songs, singing and making music in your hearts to the Lord" (Ephesians 5:18–19).

  When we completely turn our lives over to God, He comes into our spirit and lives there. Make sure you have welcomed His presence into your life.

TRAINING TIP

Sports training is not just about working out and drills. It's also about our patterns of sleep and nutrition. In the same way, what is in our minds influences how we act—so it's crucial that we provide our thought life with positive nourishment. Do you have a good mental diet?

GAME PLAN

What negative words and images do you allow to enter your mind and soul on a consistent basis? What is one thing you need to avoid? Ask God to help you stay away from that thought pattern and also ask Him to fill your mind with new thoughts.

Don't stop there. Make a commitment to begin each day with five minutes of scripture and prayer.

PRAYER

Heavenly Father, help me to think about the world the same way You do—with love and compassion and purity.

YOUR SERVE

> If I, your Lord and Teacher, have washed your feet, you also should wash each other's feet. I did this as an example so that you should do as I have done for you.
>
> JOHN 13:14-15

The coach of my tennis team had us do something quite different for practice one day this week. Instead of putting us through drills and practice matches, she loaded us into the school van and took us to an after-school program for children. She encouraged us to be there for the kids and help them with their homework or just play with them. I'll admit I didn't have a very good attitude on the drive over. My backhand needs all the help it can get. But on the drive back to school, I was the happiest I've been in a long time. It was even nice to get a break from worrying about my backhand!

—Courtney, age 16

Jesus's disciples seemed to wonder a lot about who was His favorite. In fact, two of the disciples, James and John, asked their mother to help them get the seats of honor in Jesus's kingdom. She asked Jesus: "Promise that one of my sons will sit at your right side and the other will sit at your left side in your kingdom" (Matthew 20:21).

Jesus's response was that she didn't know what she was asking. She and her sons were interested in the frills and benefits of power, but not the sacrifice involved. Otherwise, these sons of Zebedee could have been on Jesus's left and right when he prayed in the Garden (Matthew 26:40–46). Instead, they slept.

They could have been on His left and right when He was arrested in the Garden (Mark 14:50). Instead, they fled.

They could have been on His left and right when He hung on a cross (Matthew 15:27, Luke 23:49, John 19:16–19, 26). Instead, they stayed quietly in the crowd and then went into hiding.

When Jesus taught His disciples the true meaning of greatness, He taught with a towel and basin. He washed their feet—the duty of a house servant. Peter, still unable to comprehend the object lesson, initially refused to let Jesus lower Himself in such a way. But Jesus insisted that Peter learn the lesson of showing greatness by serving others.

We live in a competitive, "me-first" world. Examples of humility, kindness, helpfulness, and caring for others first—servanthood—can be hard to find. A lot of people are just out for themselves. You know many people like this.

But the truth is that the happiest and most fulfilled people are those who follow Jesus as members of the "Towel and Basin Society."

TRAINING TIP

The happiest people in the world are those who forget about themselves—their problems and worries and all the things they want—and get their minds focused on meeting the needs of others. Just as your sport requires focus, so does your spiritual life. Get your mind on others and you'll be amazed how happy you become!

GAME PLAN

Do you know a family who could use some free babysitting or a park that needs cleaning? Make arrangements to help someone in the next week. Do your best to keep your act of service between you and the person you're serving.

It's your serve. What will you do bless someone else?

PRAYER

Thank You, God, for sending Jesus into my life and heart with the gift of salvation. Help me to honor that gift through service to others.

FORGIVEN

God, be merciful to me because you are loving. Because you are always ready to be merciful, wipe out all my wrongs. Wash away all my guilt and make me clean again.

PSALM 51:1-2

I don't know why I did it, but, man, did it get me into a lot of trouble. One of my friends' parents were out of town for the weekend. When I told my parents I was staying overnight with him, I didn't tell them that his parents were gone or that a bunch of other guys were staying over to turn it into a party. Things got crazy and I ended up getting drunk. Then I got into a fight. Then we made so much noise that the police showed up. My baseball coach got all the details, and I'm serving a monthlong suspension. I may not get to play at all this season. My parents have grounded me. I'm embarrassed and feel miserable. I know I've let a lot of people down. I know I let God down most of all. I feel stupid for messing up so badly.

—Garrett, age 17

*Y*ou don't understand some of the things I've done. I'm not sure God can—or would even want to—forgive me. I've hurt my parents, my teachers, my friends, and myself.

If you've ever messed up and fallen into sin, you are not alone. Even the great heroes of the Bible had serious character flaws, sinned greatly, and were in need of God's mercy!

Jacob, the son of Isaac and one of the fathers of our faith, tricked his twin brother and even his beloved father, to "steal" the family birthright (Genesis 25–27).

Moses, who led the Hebrew slaves from the pharaoh's oppression in Egypt, murdered a man and lived as a fugitive for forty years (Exodus 2–3).

David, perhaps the most loved and popular king in Israel's history, performed many acts of courage, faith, and mercy—slaying the giant, Goliath, and sparing King Saul, a sworn enemy to him, to name just two. But he also had quite a rap sheet. His greatest crime was what he did to Uriah the Hittite, one of his bravest and most loyal soldiers. David coveted and then "took" Uriah's wife, Bathsheba. To make his evil act even worse, he had Uriah killed to try to cover up what he had done. (See II Samuel 11–12 for the whole story.)

Throughout Psalms, and especially in Psalm 51, David cried for God's mercy. He knew that being the king wouldn't get him off the hook for the bad he had done. He knew that "I'm sorry" wouldn't undo his evil deeds. But David did understand that God is merciful and will forgive the person who repents of their sins.

There is no sin so great that God's grace is not greater. Be assured that God's mercy can and will enter a darkened heart and make it pure again.

If you have behaved badly, repent, make what amends you can, and commit yourself to the task of behaving better next time. Believe God's Word when you read: "But if we confess our sins to God, He can always be trusted to forgive us and take our sins away" (I John 1:9).

TRAINING TIP

After a big win or a big loss, it is great to celebrate—or feel miserable—for a set period of time. Like until midnight of when the win or loss happened. But then it's time to move on and get ready for the next game. You won't play well if you're still thinking about the previous game. In the same way, once God forgives us of our sin, it is time to move on. God does not want us to wallow in past deeds. He wants us to move confidently into the future.

GAME PLAN

If there are past sins that have haunted you—and you have truly asked God's forgiveness—then it is time to move on. Maybe a symbolic act will help make forgiveness more real to you. Write down that thing—or those things—on a sheet of paper and place it in your fireplace (or another safe spot). Say a short prayer of thanksgiving for God's mercy, and then light the paper on fire. Let that act symbolize God's scattering your sins as far as the east is from the west.

If God moves on from your sins, so can you!

PRAYER

Heavenly Father, thank You for saving my soul, for forgiving me of my sins, and for giving me a new life in You.

DEPENDENCE ON HIM

Trust the LORD with all your heart, and
don't depend on your own understanding.
Remember the LORD in all you do,
and he will give you success.
PROVERBS 3:5-6

I'm working as hard as I can on everything
from schoolwork to being a tutor for
young girls to being the best basketball
player I can be. One of the things that is
driving me out of my mind is my free-throw
shooting. How in the world can I have a
good percentage from behind the three-point
line but I'm barely hitting 50 percent of my
free throws? My coach says I'm thinking
too much and making it more difficult than
it is. But I don't know any other way to get
things done than to focus and work harder.
I've been raised to give life my best. That's
all I'm trying to do.

—Leslie, age 18

We've been taught the value of responsibility. That's a great lesson. Work hard. Do the right thing all the time.

And, yes, being responsible is a very good thing. But when our attitude reaches the point where we trust in ourselves more than we trust in God, we can fall into one of two temptations, both of which lead to spiritual shipwreck.

The first temptation is pride, an unhealthy arrogance that slips (or roars) into our thinking when things are going great in our lives. We become convinced that we are in control of our own world and responsible for all our success.

The second temptation, hopelessness, works itself into our hearts when we face the difficulties of life that are outside of our control—an illness, a difficult relationship, or some other situation we can't fix through hard work.

Daily trusting in God—acknowledging that He is the true Source of all good gifts and success and the only safe refuge when life is difficult—steers us from the twin dangers of pride and despair.

James points out that trials test and prove our faith (James 1:1–3), but we don't have to wait for challenging moments to begin trusting God with our entire life. The good news is that with complete and total trust in Him, He directs our steps in the most fulfilling paths for our lives.

Yes, there are times in life when we need to put forth better effort. We need to try harder. Our spiritual life deserves and demands our very best. But ultimately, everything we are and can accomplish comes from God. His message to us is not to try harder but to trust more.

Are you trusting God as the Giver of all good gifts in your life?

TRAINING TIP

Rest is a big part of athletic success. If you don't get a good night's sleep, if you don't give your body time to heal up, your performance will suffer. God wants us to work for Him, but he also wants us to rest in Him.

GAME PLAN

Do an extra Bible reading today. Work slowly through Hebrews 11 in your New Testament, which provides a list of Old Testament characters who completely trusted God—against all odds. Now think of two or three of the most difficult moments in the last few years of your life. Did you face those times with faith in God? If not, how would faith have made a positive difference?

As you hit the sack tonight, talk to God about trusting Him in all your situations of life. Ask Him to give you the rest of peace.

PRAYER

Dear God, I give to You every difficulty and fear that I'm facing—along with every success and good thing—and trust You to provide the strength and grace I need to trust You in every area of my life.

LOVE AND RESPECT

Even much water cannot put out the flame of love; floods cannot drown love. If a man offered everything in his house for love, people would totally reject it.

SONG OF SOLOMON 8:7

My travel soccer club has a boys' team and a girls' team. A lot of times we go to the same tournaments and end up staying at the same hotel. So some of my best friends are on the boys' team. Recently I've been talking to one guy in particular a lot. It's pretty obvious that he is interested in me. To be honest, I'm interested in him too. My problem is that he has a pretty wild reputation. I know he doesn't go to church and he isn't interested in spiritual things like I am. I worry that if we dated, he would be bad for my spiritual life. But I also wonder if I could help him become a Christian if we dated.

—Abby, age 17

Dating can be a wonderful opportunity to interact with the opposite sex. We can learn to communicate better; we can experience careful and appropriate levels of affection; we can discover the characteristics we would like to find in a marriage partner and develop these characteristics in ourselves.

Dating can also be a horrible way to interact with the opposite sex. We can get caught up in a possessive and jealous relationship; we can lose our innocence by becoming too physical; we can obsess about the opposite sex and lose out on friendships and activities.

Before you begin dating someone, consider the following:

- You are not abnormal or weird for choosing to wait to date. You have the rest of your life to be with someone. In Ecclesiastes 3:1, Solomon said: "There is a time for everything, and everything on earth has its special season."

- Your best preparation for a future relationship is how you communicate with members of the opposite sex now. If your dating patterns are not based on positive models of communication—listening, sharing, mutual encouragement, problem solving—you are better off just being friends. "Do not stir up nor awaken love until it pleases" (Song of Solomon 8:4 NKJV).

- We need to honor God with all of ourselves, including our relationships. One of the most important elements of any relationship is respecting and valuing what is important to that person. If the person you want to date doesn't value your relationship with God, that's a pretty good indicator that the relationship is not going to honor God or help you grow closer to Him. "You are not the same as those who do not believe. So do not join yourselves to them" (2 Corinthians 6:14).

- Don't forget your parents. Even though your parents are asking you to make more and more of your own decisions, don't leave them out of what you're thinking and feeling. Ask them questions. "Honor your father and your mother" (Exodus 20:12).

God has a wonderful plan for your life. Don't try to rush it when you feel the surge of emotions from someone you are attracted to. The right person will appear to you—at the right time.

TRAINING TIP

How you train today matters right now but also impacts future performance. How we interact with members of the opposite sex impacts our state of mind now as well as how we handle future relationships.

GAME PLAN

Here are five questions you can use to evaluate your dating relationships—or whether you are even ready for a dating relationship!

- What is my motivation for dating?
- Is the person I am dating a Christian?
- Is my dating life built on sexual purity?
- Am I a positive impact on the person I'm dating? Are they a positive impact on me?
- Does my dating relationship please God?

Make a commitment to treat members of the opposite sex with love and respect.

PRAYER

Father God, I know You want what's best for me. Please guide all my decisions and relationships—and help me become the kind of person who has a positive impact on others. Amen.

RECONCILIATION

May the Lord make your love grow more and multiply for each other and for all people so that you will love others as we love you.

I THESSALONIANS 3:12

Melanie and I grew up on the same block and were best friends for as long as I can remember. The fact that we've played volleyball together since we were in the fifth grade made us even closer. We played J V in ninth grade. We both made Varsity our sophomore year. Now that we're juniors, both of us are starting. But our relationship has fallen apart. And the stupid thing is that it's because of a guy. I told Melanie that I had a crush on Dustin, and one week later they were going steady. I never actually dated him, but it hurt my feelings and I said some pretty harsh things to Melanie. She said some harsh things back and we haven't talked since, which is almost impossible since we play on the same team. I'm still hurt, but I wish I knew how to make things right between Melanie and me.

—Kelly, age 16

Jesus tells His disciples: "If you forgive anyone his sins, they are forgiven" (John 20:23). In the Lord's Prayer, He teaches us: "Forgive us for our sins, just as we have forgiven those who sinned against us" (Matthew 6:12).

One of the most important spiritual issues in God's eyes is reconciliation. Just as He sent His Son Jesus into the world to reconcile people to Himself (Colossians 1:20–22), so He gives us the mandate to be peacemakers, to be reconciled even to our enemies (Matthew 5:44).

But you don't know how that friend betrayed me. My brother doesn't care about me at all. My sister always knifes me in the back.

Obviously, one person can't do all the work when it comes to making peace. That's why we are told to keep the peace "as much as depends on you" (Romans 12:18 NKJV). But before ignoring the call to reconcile with an "enemy" as too hard, too painful, or completely unrealistic, we need to remember:

- Reconciliation is God's idea and His way of doing things (Romans 5:8-10).

- Reconciliation is tied to our relationship with God—He wants us to come before Him with right relationships (Matthew 5:23).

- As we forgive others, God forgives us (Luke 6:37).

- One of the blessings of walking with God is peace (Galatians 5:22).

What if I try to reconcile with someone and they don't respond positively?

- Reconciliation does not always happen all at once, but can take place over years, so don't give up when you don't see results right away (Galatians 6:9).

- Reconciliation does not mean we let others abuse us. Even Jesus told His disciples to "shake the dust from your feet" and avoid certain people (Matthew 10:14 CEV).

- Even when forgiveness is given both ways, sometimes we can't make a relationship exactly the way it used to be.

- Reconciliation should always be our goal. As Paul said: "Bear with each other, and forgive each other. If someone does wrong to you, forgive that person because the Lord forgave you" (Colossians 3:13).

TRAINING TIP

Reconciliation is not all up to you. The other person may reject your efforts to reconcile. You may not know how to get started. That doesn't mean you shouldn't try. The key is to trust God. With His help, even the most damaged relationships can be restored.

GAME PLAN

Who is someone with whom your relationship is strained or broken? How serious is the cause of the separation? What makes it hardest for you to seek forgiveness and reconciliation? What is one small step you can take today?

Are you ready? Say a prayer and get started now!

PRAYER

Thank You, God, that when I was far away from You and lost, You ventured to seek me out. Give me the courage to be a peacemaker in my world.

A HELPING HAND

We must not become tired of doing good. We will receive our harvest of eternal life at the right time if we do not give up.
GALATIANS 6:9

I'm one of the lucky guys. My dad and I were best friends. He worked with me on all my sports and was always there for me. I don't think that's real common these days. When he told me he was diagnosed with cancer, I felt like I couldn't breathe. I couldn't believe what was happening to him and to my family. When he passed, I was in a fog half the time and ready to start a fight the other half. I don't know how I would have gotten through that first year if it wasn't for the guys on my baseball team. And my coach. He had a lot of patience with me. Some of the guys talked to me about the loss and some just hung out and made sure I had someone around. One of my best friends always told me he was praying for me. It made all the difference in the world for me.

—Keeton, age 15

In the sixth chapter of Galatians, Paul sets out some of the most practical principles found anywhere in the Bible for expressing love to others. But just because they're practical doesn't mean they're easy!

First, he tells us that we should be redemptive people, helping restore those who have been caught in a sin (v. 1). He does caution you that as you reach out to help someone, be extra careful not to get trapped in sin yourself.

Second, Paul challenges us to love others unconditionally, without judgment or comparisons (v. 4). Competition can be friendly and healthy, but when it consumes our relationships, the inevitable result is conflict. How many friendships and sibling relationships have been torpedoed by a spirit of striving rather than a spirit of pulling together?

Next, Paul urges us to help carry the "excessive weights" that others are forced to bear (v. 2). He does point out that each of us should carry our own "backpacks," so we aren't required to do everything for others (v. 5). But when someone has burdens that are bigger than any one person should handle alone, we are to step in help.

Most importantly, Paul reminds us not to give up on loving others (v. 9). Sure, some people are unbelievably difficult to love, but if we don't lose faith in God's power to authentically change their lives, our steadfast persistence may be the very thing that makes the difference between them finding God's forgiveness and peace or never receiving God's grace in their hearts.

The result of how we relate to others is simple, according to Paul. He says, "People harvest only what they plant" (v. 7). When we sow love into others, we will ultimately receive love in return.

TRAINING TIP

You can't play baseball wearing two catcher's mitts. You have to have a free hand to throw something back. In life, it's not just about receiving. We need to be generous in helping others.

GAME PLAN

You'll never be happy just looking out for your own needs. Is there someone at your school, in your neighborhood, or on your team who is going through a really tough time and carrying a heavy load? Ask God to impress upon your heart what you can give to bless a friend who is going through a tough situation.

Even if you don't have words of encouragement, just "being there" can be exactly what someone needs!

PRAYER

Lord God, You bless me in so many ways. Help me bless others the way You have blessed me—help me see others with Your eyes.

OBEDIENCE

Mary said, "I am the servant of the Lord. Let this happen to me as you say!"
LUKE 1:38

I don't think of myself as rebellious, but it's hard for me to do things if they don't make sense to me. I've gotten into trouble at school for not doing assignments that seemed like nothing more than busywork to me. That feels like a waste of time. Of course, I got a few zeroes because of it, so I know I have no choice in the matter. Sometimes I get into trouble with my cross-country coach, too. I don't understand why she wants us to lift weights or do agility drills. Our sport is simple. Run 5K through the woods as fast as you can. I'm working on having a better attitude. But I still don't know why I need to do 20 push-ups before and after every run!

—John, age 14

Our natural inclination is not always to be obedient. All of us, at times, want to do things our way and not follow the instructions of others.

Mary, the mother of Jesus, is the best known of all the women of the Bible—people across the world know who she was and honor her. It was to Mary that God first revealed His specific plan to "save his people from their sins" through her Son (Matthew 1:21).

Mary was an ordinary young woman, engaged to a carpenter named Joseph, until one day, an angel suddenly appeared and said, "Greetings! The Lord has blessed you and is with you" (Luke 1:28), changing her life forever. The angel told her that she had been chosen to carry Jesus, the Savior of the world.

Mary could have asked a lot of questions—"What will Joseph think?" "What will happen to us?" "Am I even ready to be a mother?"

If Mary was thinking these questions, she didn't say so. She never argued or said, "Let me think this over." She simply said yes to God's plan. Her response was simple and powerful: "Let this happen to me as you say!" (Luke 1:38). She placed her reputation, her marriage, and her entire life at risk to be obedient to God—and trusted that His will was perfect.

And because of her trust and obedience, salvation became available to all humanity.

Mary's simple faith and readiness to do God's will brought the blessing of God into her life—and that same faith and obedience will bless your life today.

TRAINING TIP

Some athletes go through the motions in practice. They are never looked up to as a leader by others. Whether you know it or not, you're always being watched in life. And the things you do—by design or by accident—powerfully communicate your convictions about right and wrong, about morality and spirituality. If you want to share your faith and values with others, you must demonstrate those values in your own life.

GAME PLAN

Second Chronicles 7:14 says "Then if my people, who are called by my name, will humble themselves, if they will pray and seek me and stop their evil ways, I will hear them from heaven. I will forgive their sin, and I will heal their land."

Write out your own prayer of humble repentance, asking God to forgive areas of disobedience and help you make any changes in your life that need to be made.

PRAYER

Father God, help me to remember that Your will is good, pleasing, and perfect. Thank You so much that You reward those who do what's right. I pray that Your will would be done in my life every day. Help me to humbly follow You.

IT'S ALL ABOUT HEART

The Father has loved us so much that we are called children of God. And we really are his children.

I JOHN 3:1

My dad always wanted me to be in sports. He made sure I had the right gear, whether I was playing volleyball or soccer or softball. When one of my soccer coaches had to quit because his wife got sick, my dad stepped in and became our coach—even though he had never played soccer in his life. I appreciated all he did for me, but there was a period when I got tired of always being on a team. When I told my dad I wanted to quit soccer, he said that was my choice, but I had to finish the season. He said I couldn't be a quitter. I'm so glad he made me finish the season. I ended up having my best year ever and couldn't wait for the next season to begin.

—Trisha, age 13

If you grew up attending church, maybe you remember singing a song about a small man named Zacchaeus: "Zacchaeus was a wee little man, oh, a wee little man was he. So he climbed up in a sycamore tree for the Lord he wanted to see."

We don't know a lot about Zacchaeus's background, but we do know he was a small man—and not just because of his height. Like the Grinch from the Dr. Seuss book, what was truly small was his heart. A corrupt tax collector, he stole from his own people on behalf of the Roman government that ruled his people, and as a result, just about everyone he knew despised him as much as he despised them.

But apparently, deep in his soul, Zacchaeus wanted something more—something bigger—in his life. He didn't want more money. He wanted to love and to be loved. That all became possible when Jesus entered his life.

He opened his home to Jesus, inviting Him and people he once despised to dinner. Something happened to him. He accepted Jesus into his heart and everything changed. Unlike the rich young ruler who loved money more than people, Zacchaeus opened his pocketbook and paid people back even more than he had stolen from them. Most of all, he opened his heart to the life-changing power of God's love. And like the Grinch, his heart grew three sizes in a miraculous moment in time.

The question is never whether God loves you. The real question is whether you will open your heart and receive that love. Your life, your soul, your heart will grow bigger than they could ever be without Him.

"I Hope You Dance" is a famous song that is still played years after Lee Ann Womack first recorded it. One of the lines people love is: "And when you get the choice to sit it out or dance, I hope you dance."

Do you say yes to God's love in your heart and life? When invited to the divine dance, are you sitting down or responding to the offer of love?

Being a Christian isn't about doing certain things and being religious. It is a relationship. It is personally knowing God through Jesus Christ. Say yes to God's incredible invitation to know Him deep in your heart.

TRAINING TIP

The best athletes don't just "do" their sport; they "love" their sport. It gives them the drive to work hard when others are taking it easy. It helps them overcome difficulties and come out a winner. Don't follow God because of guilt or fear. Fall in love with the Savior who died for you!

GAME PLAN

Do you ever feel like quitting? That's okay. Playing a sport is not the most important thing in life. You may be at a point where other activities are more important to you. Simply ask yourself the question, Am I putting my heart into it? After answering that, you can make your decision.

But whatever you are doing right now, commit yourself to giving it your all.

PRAYER

Dear heavenly Father, thank You so much for Your love. God, please come and fill my heart with love and enthusiasm today. Most of all, help me to live for you with all my heart, soul, and strength.

ROLE MODELS

**Follow my example,
as I follow the example of Christ.**
I CORINTHIANS 11:1

I always wanted to be like my big brother. He was great at every sport he did. His junior year he took third place in the state wrestling tournament in the 132-pound class. I was still in middle school, but that fired me up to work even harder. The next year, Dan got in with the wrong crowd. I don't know all he got into, but he ended up getting suspended from school, and he got kicked off the team. That was the hardest thing I've ever seen. I still remember him looking at me and sticking a finger in my face and saying, "Little bro, if you ever get into the kind of trouble I am in, I'm going to be the first person to kick your butt back into shape." He's doing well now, but it still makes me sad that he missed his senior year of wrestling. He's in college now, but I believe he'll keep his promise and get in my face if I get into trouble. I guess that makes him a good big brother.

—Greg, age 14

Who are the influencers in your life? Who has the biggest impact on you?

We don't know much about Paul's student Timothy from his own words. But from Paul's letters written to him in the New Testament, we discover that Timothy deeply appreciated his godly heritage (1 Timothy 1:4), he carefully followed the teaching of his mentor, Paul (1 Timothy 1:19), and as a result, he was wise beyond his years as a minister and leader (1 Timothy 4:12). Timothy had great influence because of the person who influenced him.

If you want to be a great leader, you must be willing to be a great follower—to choose the right role models and learn from them. An exhausted, ineffective, frustrated Moses could not keep up with the demands of leading his people—until he listened to the counsel of his father-in-law (Exodus 18:24). That takes humility and courage!

Bottom line, we would all do better if we had a trusted mentor in our lives, and that won't happen until our hearts are open and we are humble enough to learn from someone else. Sports teach you leadership, but they also teach you the value of being a great follower!

If you want to get better grades, study with a straight-A student. If you want to improve your tennis game, play opponents who are better than you. If you want to grow spiritually, look for a friend or adult who really demonstrates spiritual grace and joy. And then pass along what you've learned to others!

There is one warning we all need to keep in mind. Just as we need positive role models in our lives, there are some people who will drag us down in our attitude and actions. In the first verse of the first psalm, David tells us what will make us happy: "God blesses those people who refuse evil advice and won't follow sinners or join in sneering at God" (Psalm 1:1 CEV). We are to love and be friendly to everyone. But we can't let everyone steer the direction we should go.

The question is, who do you look to as a role model? Who do you allow the most influence in your life?

TRAINING TIP

When you really listen to and follow the instructions of a great coach, it will make you better in your sport. To reach our full potential in our spiritual lives, we all need someone to look up to and learn from.

GAME PLAN

What is one area of your life where you know you need a little help to become all that you can be? Write that down on an index card. Now list names of several people who have something to teach you in this area—a youth leader or a teacher, a coach, a friend or a sibling.

Pray for these people over the next week and ask God to lead you to the person—whether or not they are on the list—who can help you go to the next level.

PRAYER

Dear heavenly Father, thank You that You take an interest in Your children's growth and development as people. Please show me ways to grow and who can help me, along with who I can help in return.

JEALOUSY

Each person should judge his own actions and not compare himself with others. Then he can be proud for what he himself has done.

GALATIANS 6:4

I feel like a lousy teammate, but I can't seem to help it. I'm so tired of Jake getting all the attention. We've been friends forever, but it seems like he is a different person than the guy I grew up with. No doubt, he is a great quarterback. He's got great talent, and he works hard. But ever since he started getting recruited by a bunch of big colleges, it seems like he feels he is too good for the rest of us. I play center on the offensive line, so I know I'm not going to get a lot of attention—unless I make a mistake and have a bad snap. But it feels like Jake is taking me and everyone else for granted. He got sacked last game and was snapping at all of us in the huddle. I know I shouldn't feel jealous and complain about him, but right now that's how I feel.

—Zach, age 17

Have you ever been bitten by the green-eyed monster called jealousy? When we let jealousy creep or roar into our souls, we hurt ourselves—including our relationship with God—and we hurt others in a number of ways:

- We let competition come before relationships: "Let us walk properly, as in the day, not in revelry and drunkenness, not in lewdness and lust, not in strife and envy" (Romans 13:13 NKJV). Sure it's good to do our best. We want good grades. We want to win at tennis. We want to strive for excellence, and sometimes that means competition. But when we let competition dominate our relationships, strife and hurt feelings will always be the result.

- We let comparisons sour relationships: "Each person should judge his own actions and not compare himself with others. Then he can be proud for what he himself has done" (Galatians 6:4). If God created you the way you are for a reason—if He loves you for who you are; if He has a plan and purpose for your life; why would you want to be like someone else? It's almost the same as saying others have a better idea for your life than God does.

- We let criticizing and complaining control our attitudes toward others: "Do everything without complaining or arguing" (Philippians 2:14). If you find yourself constantly criticizing others, guess what? They might not be the real problem. The real problem might be your feelings of jealousy. What causes jealousy? Often it is feelings of inferiority. No wonder Jesus says "Love your neighbor as you love yourself" [Matthew 22:39]. Once we love ourselves, we no longer feel the need to trash others.

Jealousy is the fear that you do not have value. Jealousy worries that others will be preferred and rewarded more than you. There is only one antidote to jealousy, and that is to affirm that God loves you for who you are and has a wonderful plan for your life. It might not mean that you are the star quarterback or the number one singles player in tennis or best shooter in basketball. But it is just right for you.

When we love ourselves as God loves us, we can slay the green-eyed monster of jealousy.

TRAINING TIP

Great teams have great stars and great role players. Every single player is needed for a successful season. The same is true in life. Maybe you are a star or maybe you contribute in other ways. The important thing is for you to affirm that you are essential to the success of your family, your community, and your team.

GAME PLAN

The best antidote to jealousy is to affirm your belief in God and that He has a purpose for you. As you let your soul find rest in Him, you'll find that you compare yourself with others less and less. Sit down and make a list of the things that make you unique and a contributor in the world.

Place your list in a place where you'll see it often as a reminder not to compare yourself to others, but to be the best "you" you can be.

PRAYER

Lord God, please forgive me for allowing jealousy to take hold of my heart and hurt my relationships. Please help me to find my strength in You today and to bless the people around me.

NO PREJUDICE

This is what the Lord All-Powerful says: "Do what is right and true. Be kind and merciful to each other."
ZECHARIAH 7:9

The school I go to is very multicultural. We have a few problems with fighting, but it seems to me that the real problem is everyone sticking with their own group. Our whole school is filled with tribes that have no interest in getting to know anyone different. I'm on the basketball team. I guess you'd call that my tribe. We're different colors and backgrounds, but we all get along pretty good. The other day after practice, a couple of us were talking about our school. Is it even possible to break down barriers between race and other superficial things that divide us? One of my friends on the team says that things will always stay the way they are. I'd like to do something but don't know where to start. Is he right?

—Tanner, age 16

Some religious leaders challenged Jesus with a question about who we should consider our neighbor. In other words, who was acceptable and who was unacceptable?

Jesus gave them an answer, but not to the question they asked. Instead of telling them who their neighbor was, He told them what a good neighbor looks like, through the powerful story of the Good Samaritan.

Note, many Jewish leaders of Jesus's day would have nothing to do with Samaritans, so you can imagine how mad they were that Jesus made a Samaritan the hero of the story—and the model for kindness.

In taking care of a fellow traveler who had been beaten and robbed, the Samaritan teaches us that:

- Kindness can be costly: "The next day, the Samaritan brought out two coins, gave them to the innkeeper, and said, 'Take care of this man. If you spend more money on him, I will pay it back to you when I come again' " (Luke 10:35). No question, kindness requires effort—and sometimes even sacrifice on our part.

- Kindness can be risky: "Evil people will not learn to do good even if you show them kindness" (Isaiah 26:10). Just as the Samaritan man risked being mugged himself by slowing down to help someone who had been beaten, at times our kindness will be taken advantage of. Is it worth the risk? Jesus says yes!

- Kindness turns enemies into friends: "The Samaritan went to him, poured olive oil and wine on his wounds, and bandaged them. Then he put the hurt man on his own donkey and took him to an inn where he cared for him" (Luke 10:34). If this Jew and Samaritan could be united through kindness, what might happen to your relationships as you become a good neighbor?

- Kindness blesses people's lives and helps them change: "A smiling king can give people life; his kindness is like a spring shower" (Proverbs 16:15). Peter writes to the church: "Most importantly, love each other deeply, because love will cause people to forgive each other for many sins" (I Peter 4:8).

There are countless teens at your school who have all but given up on a good God because of how they've been mistreated. You have friends on your team who need your kindness as well.

You can change their perspective with kindness. Too often we underestimate the power of a touch, a smile, a kind word, a listening ear, an honest compliment, or the smallest act of caring, all of which have the potential to turn a life around.

Who can you be a neighbor to today?

TRAINING TIP

Our world is filled with distrust and strife due to real or perceived prejudices. Sports is one place where people come together as players and fans. Share the love of God by demonstrating your love for all people. Kill hatred with kindness.

GAME PLAN

A movement that has been quite popular is called Random Acts of Kindness. There was even a day of the year dedicated to going above and beyond in a lavish act of goodness toward others. Though kindness can't just be for a day, we must start somewhere.

Pick a day this week and plot out three or four kind deeds you will do for family members and friends at school. Have a lot of fun with this activity and make someone's day!

PRAYER

God, thank You so much for Your kindness to me and the kindness shown to me by so many people. Help me be an instrument of Your kindness to someone today.

WISE DECISIONS

> If you go the wrong way—to the right or to the left—you will hear a voice behind you saying, "This is the right way. You should go this way."
>
> ISAIAH 30:21

I was sitting the bench on my basketball team. I felt like I was better than some of the guys who were getting all the playing time. So I got mad and quit the team. Now I'm miserable. I made a huge mistake. My mom told me to do what I can to make things right. I'm listening to her. I meet with the coach tomorrow to ask if he will let me back on the team. I have no idea what he'll say. I'm hoping and praying I get another chance.

—Jonathan, age 13

The way you make decisions will determine the kind of life you lead. Consistently make bad decisions and have a consistently hard life. Make wise decisions and live the life God planned for you. Here are a few reminders:

- Ask God for wisdom: "But if any of you needs wisdom, you should ask God for it. He is generous to everyone and will give you wisdom without criticizing you" (James 1:5). We ask God to help us with all sorts of problems. Why not ask Him for one of the greatest gifts in the world—wisdom? He wants to give this to you.

- Study God's Word: "Your word is like a lamp for my feet and a light for my path" (Psalm 119:105). Literacy rates may be going up in our culture, but biblical illiteracy is at epidemic levels. Stand out from the crowd and read God's Word every day.

- Talk to God throughout the day: "Pray continually" (I Thessalonians 5:17). We need alone time to pray in a focused way, but we also need to talk to God as if He was with us in every situation—because He is with us in every situation.

- Seek smart peer pressure: "Spend time with the wise and you will become wise, but the friends of fools will suffer" (Proverbs 13:20). Get close to people who live their lives and make the kinds of decisions you want for yourself. Be kind and friendly to everyone. But make sure you interact with wise people every day. As David reminds us: "Happy are those who don't listen to the wicked, who don't go where sinners go, who don't do what evil people do. They love the LORD's teachings, and they think about those teachings day and night (Psalm 1:1–2).

- Correct your mistakes: "My dear children, I write this letter to you so you will not sin. But if anyone does sin, we have a helper in the presence of the Father—Jesus Christ, the One who does what is right" (I John 2:1). If you do make a bad choice, don't compound it by staying the course. Swallow your pride. Apologize. Ask forgiveness. Make an immediate U-turn.

Though no one can go back and make a brand-new start, anyone can start from now and make a brand-new ending. What kind of ending are you building for your life?

TRAINING TIP

No one is perfect in sports. Everyone misses shots, strikes out, commits a stupid penalty, misses a blocking assignment, or makes some other mistake. What makes a player great is when they learn from their mistakes and corrects themselves to improve. The same is true in all of life. We will all fail. The question is whether we learn and grow from failure.

GAME PLAN

What are the five dumbest decisions you have made this year? Don't make a list to wallow in self-pity and feel defeated. Simply look at each decision and ask yourself, how can I make a better decision next time?

Now ask God to give you the wisdom and power to make great decisions today and throughout your teen years as an athlete, and, more importantly, as a person with a great future ahead of you.

PRAYER

Father God, sometimes it scares me to realize how much impact my decisions have on my life. Thanks for being there to advise me—and thanks that my life is in Your hands.

THE POWER OF PRAYER

Pray in the Spirit at all times with all kinds of prayers, asking for everything you need. To do this you must always be ready and never give up. Always pray for all God's people.
EPHESIANS 6:18

I have no complaints in life. I'm getting along well with my parents. I'm doing pretty good in school. I'm having a blast on my swim team. We all get along, we're doing well in meets, and I absolutely love my coach. I'm not the best, but I've been improving every year and feel like I'm doing the best I can. I've been a Christian for a long time. I believe in God and want to live for Him. But I do feel like should be further along in my Christian life than I am. It's easy to know I'm improving in the pool because the clock doesn't lie. But I'm having a hard time seeing growth in my spiritual life. I know God loves me. I haven't lost my faith. But I want more. One area where I know I need help is in my prayer life. I try to pray, but sometimes I feel like I'm talking to myself.

—Courtney, age 17

At the beginning of His ministry at age thirty, despite having so much to do in such a short amount of time for His Father in heaven, Jesus pulled away from everyone to spend forty days in the wilderness to pray and fast. While alone, Jesus was tested three times by Satan, but each time He answered the challenge with scripture and a profound sense of His purpose in life (Matthew 4:1–11).

Again, at the end of his earthly life, Jesus pulled away from the crowds to pray alone in the Garden of Gethsemane (Mark 14:35–36). It was there, with the agony of the cross just before Him, that He re-affirmed His most earnest desire: "Not My will, but Yours, be done" (Luke 22:42 NKJV).

If Jesus Christ spent time in personal prayer, how much more important is it for us? We can come to the end of the day—or week or even month—and discover that we have made little or no time at all to be alone with God. Television, music, schoolwork, practices, and other "noises" compete for our time and attention.

Jesus told His disciples, "If you ask me for anything in my name, I will do it" (John 14:14). Prayer is powerful. It doesn't change God, but it does change us. One of the ways we learn to pray is to pray as Jesus prayed. His prayers often came straight from scripture. But at the heart of His prayers, He wanted to honor His Heavenly Father: "Your will be done."

There is no better way to grow closer to God than spending time in prayer and silent reflection, taking time to really hear God's voice. God changes you when you spend time with Him. He guides you, letting you know that He wants to use you to do something big in your life. He's most likely to be able to communicate that to you if you're spending regular time in prayer (John 15:4).

You don't have to take a forty-day trip to the desert to spend quiet time with God. You can choose today to make prayer a higher priority in your life. As you ask God to help you, He will prosper your prayer life—and your soul.

TRAINING TIP

Have you ever had a coach yell to the team during a time-out or practice, "Hey, listen up!" God is saying the same thing to us. We get distracted and confused and lose our way, but He stays with us and calls for us to "Listen up"!

GAME PLAN

If Jesus prayed from scripture, then that is obviously something we should do too. The Psalms are known as the "prayer book" of the Bible. Pick out a favorite psalm, maybe starting with chapter 1. Read the psalm slowly and carefully and then put it in your own words as a prayer to God.

Since we know God's Word reveals His will for our lives, praying from scripture means we will always be praying for what He wants most in our lives.

PRAYER

You speak to me through Your Word and through pastors and through books, but thank You, God, that You speak to me in a quiet voice when I am silent before You. Thank You for the wonderful gift of prayer.

YOU ARE LOVED

The LORD did not care for you and choose you because there were many of you—you are the smallest nation of all. But the LORD chose you because he loved you, and he kept his promise to your ancestors.

Deuteronomy 7:7–8

I love playing on the tennis team. But I'm definitely not the best player on my team. And I lose more than I win. Whenever I lose a match, I feel bad about myself. It makes me feel like a loser. Sometimes I want to quit because then I wouldn't feel so bad about myself. I always feel like there is something wrong with me. I don't feel good about myself. I work as hard as everyone else. Actually, I work harder than most of the guys on my team. I'm just not as good. I don't think that's going to change. Is it better for me if I don't play sports at all?

—Kevin, age 14

If ever there was a person who had reasons to struggle with self-image, it was the woman who met Jesus at the well as recorded in John 4.

- First of all, she was a Samaritan. In Jesus's day, the Jews despised all Samaritans as religious infidels and "half-breeds." When Israel was conquered by the Babylonians in 586 BC, the youngest and most educated were taken into captivity. When their descendants returned to Jerusalem seventy years later, they expected to find a thriving center of worship and faith. Instead, many who had been left behind converted to other religions and married people from other countries. They were despised from that moment on.

- Second, she was a woman, which meant she had second-class status in that day and age. In her culture she was viewed as the "property" of her husband.

- Third, she had failed at love. Jesus asked her where her husband was. She admitted that she wasn't married but was living with a man. Jesus pointed out she had previously been married five times! Whether a serial widow or divorcée, she had probably given up on marital vows. She no longer viewed herself as worthy to be loved.

- Fourth, she was rejected by her peers. Jesus met her during the hottest time of the day with no one else around her. The women of Middle East villages gathered water at the well together during the coolest part of the day.

If anyone had reason to feel bad about themselves and their lot in life, it was this Samaritan woman. But when Jesus entered her life, everything changed. He took the initiative and spoke to her first, uncommon for a man to do in that culture. In the same way, He reaches out to us long before we reach toward Him. He looked at her as a person on the basis of her potential—not her past or even her present circumstances. Most importantly, He offered her a living water that would satisfy the emptiness and longing of her soul, a drink of water that would provide renewal for her parched soul and life.

Even if you lose a match, even if you feel as needy as a lonely Samaritan at a well today—be assured that Jesus provides you with all the reasons you need to love and embrace yourself.

TRAINING TIP

Winning and losing is how we judge our athletic career. But God judges us on our faithfulness to Him. When God sees someone as truly successful, He sees someone who is giving all they have to Him.

GAME PLAN

Sometimes we do our best thinking when we write things down. Write a letter to yourself, reminding you of how much God loves you—and your own sense of self-appreciation. Tuck it somewhere safe so that no matter what is happening in your life, you have a reminder of how much you are loved.

God knows you best and loves you most. Never forget that truth!

PRAYER

Thank You, God, for being the One who believes in me and loves me as no one else ever could. You see into my heart and declare me as something special and incredible. Thank You for loving me so much.

THE SECRET OF BEING HAPPY

[Remember] the words the Lord Jesus himself said: "It is more blessed to give than to receive."

ACTS 20:35 NIV

My friend Sophia pulled a hamstring during the first game of the season. She tried to turn a double into a triple. Halfway to third base, she stood straight up. She tried hobbling to the bench but two of our coaches ended up carrying her off the field. She has been hurting and struggling all season. About the time she thinks she is completely good to go, she ends up tweaking the hammy again. She has to start over with therapy. Her physical therapist gave her a series of stretches to do at home. I knew how miserable she was, so I volunteered to help her every day. I thought I was going to get tired of driving over to her house after supper every evening. But after a week, I discovered a couple of things. First, she really did need help. Second, I am actually a pretty good trainer. And third, the more I helped, the more I liked helping. Who knows, I may go into physical therapy as a career someday.

—Emma, age 18

One of the greatest—but most neglected—sources of experiencing joy and blessings in one's life is through bringing joy and blessing to others. Despite the various psychological and sociological studies that prove the happiest people in the world are those who serve others, volunteerism in America and throughout the world is at an all-time low.

How about you? Of course you are busy. But are you blessing others?

No question, life is filled to the brim with work, priorities, and pressures that can tap our strength, but perhaps if we reached out more, we would discover more energy and joy than we knew was possible. Jesus taught His disciples that it is more blessed to give than to receive. One obvious—but easily forgotten—reason is that if you are giving to others, it implies you have something to give in the first place!

Most of us can count many blessings in our lives right now. But can we just as easily count the number of ways that we bless others? In Deuteronomy 16, the children of Israel are reminded to come before the Lord to worship. Three yearly feasts had been established as special times to grow closer to God. Passover, the subject of chapter 16, was to be celebrated at the beginning of the year to commemorate that God had delivered Israel from oppression and slavery (Exodus 12:2). What a blessing! One of the clear expectations when the people attended the feast was spelled out in verse 16:17: As God has blessed you, bring a gift of gratitude to bless God and others.

Has God answered your prayers? It is wonderful to serve a God who wants to bless you, but let's not forget to bless others in equal measure.

TRAINING TIP

We usually get most excited about game time. There is a special energy once the game gets started. We might enjoy practice a lot, but it rarely compares to playing the actual game for excitement. One of the key sources of injury is inadequate training, particularly a lack of proper stretching. Make sure you are aware of the best ways to stretch and warm up for your sport.

GAME PLAN

If you've been injured in a game, you know how tough it is to get yourself healthy again. Therapy is usually done all by yourself. It can be painful. It is often painful. Think about one of your teammates who might be in the middle of rehab. How can you help out?

Even if it is just hanging around to let a friend know that they aren't alone, be there for others who are hurt.

PRAYER

Faithful God, thank You that when I bless others, You bless me! Thank You for the joy and happiness You bring into my life.

JUST SAY IT

For it is with your heart that you believe and are justified, and it is with your mouth that you profess your faith and are saved.
ROMANS 10:10 NIV

I've been friends with Jaxson since we were little kids. We've played for the same travel soccer club since middle school. Jaxson has always been the star of the team. But this past season, for some reason, I got a whole lot better. I've always scored some goals, but this year, I scored a bunch. More than one a game. At the end-of-the-year team banquet, I was given the trophy for team MVP. I got a lot of attention. My coach told me that he has received a couple of calls from colleges interested in watching me when high school season starts. Every single other guy on the team said something nice to me. It was a little embarrassing. But it still bothered me that Jaxson said nothing. We drove home together, and he never even brought it up. I don't know if he's jealous or what. But I've always been there to compliment him when he did great things. It never bothered me when he was the star and I was just okay.

-Chase, age 17

A woman complained that her husband never told her that he loved her. When she confronted him on that topic one day, his answer was: "I told you I loved you on the day we got married, thirty years ago. Since nothing's changed, why repeat myself?"

It's good that the husband told his wife he loved her that one time. But she longed to hear what was in his heart again. Okay, that probably never happened and is actually just a joke. But it makes a pretty clear point. A lot of us don't say out loud to others what we should. Are we embarrassed? Do we assume they already know what we're thinking? Why don't we use the words to let people know what is most important to us? Most importantly, why don't we let others know how much God loves them?

Salvation is a matter of the heart: forgiveness. It is also a matter of our actions: repentance (turning from our sinful habits). But it is also a matter of our words: confession.

We speak the words on the day that we receive Jesus Christ into our hearts, but we continue to confess what God has done and is doing in our lives as we grow in our faith.

Not all of us are called to preach. We're not all destined to be evangelists. But all of us are called to say out loud that Jesus is our Lord and Savior. We can do that through a testimony of the day we were saved or through simple expressions that acknowledge God in your heart and life. Even a statement to coworkers or neighbors like "I've been so blessed by God" can open the doors to deeper spiritual conversations at God-appointed moments.

Confession is a wonderful and powerful way to grow spiritually—and to bless others. Our words tell others—and our self—what is in our heart. What are you telling the world is in your heart?

TRAINING TIP

Not everyone has the same personality. Some people are naturally louder and more talkative. These are the ones who help fire up a team when things aren't looking good. Even if you are not a natural "cheerleader," make sure you verbally affirm and encourage others!

GAME PLAN

If you suddenly had the opportunity to tell someone how to become a Christian, would you know what to say? There are many simple "plans" to share the message of salvation with someone who is ready to pray with you. One of the simplest is the Roman Road of Salvation. You simply remember the following five verses in order. If someone is close to receiving Jesus as their Savior, you simply read through the verses and explain the spiritual principle of each one.

- Romans 3:23—all of us have sinned.
- Romans 6:23—the wages is sin is spiritual death but the gift of God is spiritual life.
- Romans 5:8—Jesus paid the price for our sins.
- Romans 10:9—when we confess Jesus is Lord of our lives, we are saved.
- Romans 5:1—with Jesus in our hearts, we have peace with God.

PRAYER

Loving Father, with my words, I declare that You are my Lord and Savior. Help me to share that wonderful experience with others.

YOU'VE GOT THE POWER

I pray that out of his glorious riches he may strengthen you with power through his Spirit in your inner being, so that Christ may dwell in your hearts through faith.

EPHESIANS 3:16-17 NIV

You should see my trophy case in our family room. It is loaded. People come over, look at all my hardware, and say that I must be an incredible basketball player. The truth is, I'm just okay. So when I tell you how many trophies I have, I'm really not bragging. The reason for all my shiny gold and silver is that for five years, I've played on an incredible travel team and school team. I mean, incredible. We've got everything. There's no team that can match our shooting, passing, rebounding, and defense. The reason I get to play as much as I do is that we always have a big lead by halftime. So when people ask me for the secret of my success, I laugh and tell them: "Play for a great team."

—Austin, age 16

A little boy came face-to-face with a bully on the playground. Instead of backing down, he stood tall and smiled. The bully threatened to punch him if he didn't hand over his lunch money. The little boy continued to smile and let the bully know, "You aren't getting my money." The bully got a smile on his face. He was going to teach this little boy a lesson. But the little boy smiled right back and reminded the bully: "You are making a big mistake by threatening me."

Both mad and confused, the bully yelled at him, "Are you crazy? Don't you know I'm going to pound you and there's nothing you can do to stop me?" The little boy pointed at an older, larger kid across the playground and said, "That's my brother. If you lay a hand on me, you're the crazy one."

That story should bring a smile to your face and serve as a reminder that it's good to have powerful friends and big brothers. There's nothing more fun in sports than to play for a powerful team.

If you want to be powerful, common logic says to look for the most powerful allies. If you are the ruler of a country, built the biggest army. If you play on a basketball team, make sure you are with the quickest point guard, the best shooters, and the strongest rebounders.

But what gets forgotten by people of all ages and in all situations in life is that no force in the universe is more powerful than God. That means when we are connected to God, we have the ultimate "big brother."

The apostle Paul prays that we would receive a power that stands in contrast to our typical definitions of strength. He prays that through our faith we would fully appreciate and receive an inner strength that resides in our heart.

Do you consider yourself to be a person of power and strength? If you have even the slightest doubt, pray along with Paul that you would receive a unique internal power that resides inside of you and permeates every fiber of your being.

It's great to play with the best players, but it's even better to live with the Lord of creation and life.

TRAINING TIP

Most sports employ both strength and conditioning in their training program. Anabolic (strength) and aerobic (endurance) training help you become your very best. Do you have a good workout regime for out-of-season and in-season strength and conditioning? Talk to your coach, other players, and trainers to find ways to improve your performance.

GAME PLAN

In sports, we learn to give our best effort and try even harder. But in our spiritual life, to do and be our very best, we don't try harder; we trust God more. He is the source of our power to live a victorious life.

Discuss with your pastor, youth leader, coach, parent, or other trusted adult what it means for them to completely trust God.

PRAYER

Father, from Your glorious riches, grant me the strength to face any challenge or temptation that I might face in life.

STOP HIDING

Let us draw near to God with a sincere heart and with the full assurance that faith brings, having our hearts sprinkled to cleanse us from a guilty conscience and having our bodies washed with pure water.

HEBREWS 10:22 NIV

I started off the season pitching great. I had no problems with control. Everything I threw was over the plate. Sure, I gave up some hits and a few runs, but overall, I was considered my team's most reliable relief pitcher. We're coming to the end of the season. Maybe my arm is tired. All I know is that batters are rocking my pitches. I gave up two home runs in the same inning during the last game. Now we are down to a few games and we're really close to winning our league and making it to the district tournament. I've always sat as close to the coach as I can. I don't want her to forget me. I want her to see me and put me in. Now I'm sitting at the far edge of the bench and making sure someone is between us so she doesn't see me. I've lost my confidence and don't know what to do.

—Violet, age 17

One of the most powerful stories in the Bible about hiding from God can be found in Genesis 3. Adam and Eve lived in the Garden of Eden, a place of safety and abundance, where their every need and wish was fully satisfied. Most wonderful of all, God personally visited with them each day in a perfect relationship. But then came the serpent, who planted seeds of doubt in their hearts that God knew what was best for them. When faced with temptation, both Adam and Eve fell in disobedience. When God came to visit the couple, He had to call out to them, because in their guilt and shame they hid from Him.

The good news for each of us is that God still calls out to us—even if we have fallen because of our sin and disobedience. Because of God's never-ending love for us, He seeks us even when we have hidden ourselves in shame.

The writer to the Hebrews makes the simple appeal that, rather than waiting for God to find us, we should seek Him out; we should do all we can to draw close to Him.

But God knows my shame. He knows my failings. I am not worthy to stand in His presence.

The good news continues. With a sincere heart filled with faith, He cleanses us from the burdens of shame and guilt so that we can approach Him with a purity we longed for but didn't think was possible. His forgiving, cleansing, loving power—His grace—provides us everything we need to come before His throne with both humility and boldness.

What are you waiting for? Are you still hiding? Now is the time to draw near to God!

TRAINING TIP

Work, work, work. Keep pushing. Try harder. Don't give up. Be the first one to arrive at practice and the last one to leave. Be the hardest worker....All that is great. But don't forget, sometimes your body needs rest. Are you getting good sleep? Do you need to go to bed earlier? Are you making sure you give your body recovery time after a hard workout?

GAME PLAN

We can go through a season where we lose our confidence in sports. Maybe we haven't been doing as well lately. Don't hide at the end of the bench. Let your coach and teammates know you are trying. Give them a chance to encourage you. In the same way, in your spiritual life, if you fail, if you sin, if you do something you know is wrong, don't run from God and others. We need each other to grow spiritually.

If you have been hiding from God, spend time in prayer, asking Him to forgive you and expressing your love for Him.

PRAYER

Almighty God, I walk into Your presence with confidence because of Your gracious invitation and your cleansing power.

LOVING THE UNLOVABLE

8

Therefore, as God's chosen people, holy and dearly loved, clothe yourselves with compassion, kindness, humility, gentleness and patience. Bear with each other and forgive one another if any of you has a grievance against someone. Forgive as the Lord forgave you.

COLOSSIANS 3:12-13 NIV

When I showed up for the first day of high school practice with the freshman team, the strangest thing for me was to be assigned a locker next to Elijah. Elijah went to a different middle school than me. We were big rivals. And I always thought Elijah was a dirty player. No one on my middle school team liked him. After the first week of no-contact practice, I learned pretty quickly that I still didn't like Elijah. He constantly takes cheap shots, even against his own teammates. I'm not sure what to do. I know I need to support my teammates. But at this point, I just can't stand Elijah.

—Mason, age 14

Every living creature has been blessed by God with a way to protect itself. When a sand particle gets inside an oyster's shell, for example, that tiny abrasive becomes life-threatening to the oyster due to the soft, porous tissue. But the oyster secretes an essence from its own life to create a pearl from the grain of sand.

What would happen if we, like the oyster, didn't try to discard the abrasive and unlovable people from our lives—even when we feel threatened—but rather welcomed them as opportunities for God's love to create something beautiful inside us? Those bothersome people might need you to help them experience God's new life. Likewise, you might need them to develop your patience and godly love. So don't automatically expel difficult people from your life; ask God to help you turn an annoyance into a pearl.

Love means to love that which is unlovable, or it is no virtue at all. Are you reaching out and showing love to the unlovable? The easy path is to ignore, avoid, and reject certain people. Perhaps there are some individuals that are so harmful to us and our loved ones that we should avoid them. But our first response needs to be compassion and love. Are you demonstrating the fruit of the Holy Spirit by showing kindness, patience, and love?

As obedience to God, are you willing to love that unlovable person on your team?

TRAINING TIP

Here's some not-so-great news. Difficult people don't disappear after you graduate from high school or college and go out into the world. Difficult people are everywhere. Some are negative. Some are obnoxious. Some are bullies. Some people need to be avoided. Some people need to be confronted. The important thing is to learn now that you can't let difficult people get under your skin or ruin your attitude about life.

GAME PLAN

In Matthew 5:44, Jesus teaches us: "But I say to you, love your enemies. Pray for those who hurt you." Is there anything harder than that? That means it is important. Maybe your prayers won't change the other person, but your prayers will change you, strengthening you on the inside.

Who is a person you just can't stand? Take time this day to pray for them, asking God to help them with any problems they have, but also making you a more loving and compassionate person.

PRAYER

Lord, I want to allow You to work in my life through any circumstances, even the unpleasant ones. Teach me to love with Your love.

INCLUDING EVERYBODY

Do not forget to entertain strangers,
for by so doing some people have
unwittingly entertained angels.
HEBREWS 13:2 NKJV

I love my gymnastics squad. Most of us grew up together. There's a new girl, Riley, who moved to town recently. She just made the team. My friends aren't crazy about her. One of my friend nicknamed her the "Ice Queen." I actually think she's okay. But she definitely needs help making friends. She's not weird or anything; she's just a little shy and doesn't seem to know how to fit in. My only concern is that I don't want to lose the friends I do have by trying to help Riley fit in.

—Amelia, age 15

If we're honest, there are people who make us feel comfortable, and there are people who make us feel uncomfortable. Some our friends' homes are warm and inviting. Some of our friends' homes just don't make us feel comfortable. It's not a matter of who has the biggest or nicest house; it is a matter of who is the most welcoming. How welcoming are you? Do you make friends feel comfortable? How about people you've just met? Do you have a welcoming spirit that helps them fit in and belong?

Throughout scripture, an act of hospitality becomes the opportunity for a holy moment. Abraham serves a meal for three strangers—and he receives a special message directly from God about his and Sarah's future (Genesis 18:1–15). The widow at Zarephath makes a cake of bread for Elijah out of the very last of her flour and oil and, miraculously, she never runs out of food supplies during a time of famine (I Kings 17:7–24). Peter's mother serves Jesus and the disciples after He heals her from a fever (Matthew 8:14–15). Zacchaeus receives the love of God through an encounter with Jesus and immediately insists that He and His disciples come to his home for a feast (Luke 19:1–10).

In our modern day, hospitality can still be something holy. God blesses us for receiving others into our homes and hearts. And when we take the time to demonstrate care for people we don't know well, we learn that we are merely returning the love God gives to us.

Have you welcomed the new teammate to your team? It's great to have friends who have been known for a long time, but are you open to making new friends and including them in your social network?

TRAINING TIP

People who are open to new knowledge, new experiences, and new people are the people who keep growing in life. This is true in sports and school and neighborhood. If you haven't made a new friend this year, it is time to open your eyes to others around you.

GAME PLAN

What is the secret of making new friends and being a person who welcomes even "strangers" into his or her world? It's not as hard as you think.

1. Be confident.
2. Don't judge people before you meet them.
3. Say "Hi" first.
4. Smile a lot.
5. Pay attention to others and be a good listener.
6. Introduce yourself and your friends to others.
7. Invite new people into your home and activities.

PRAYER

Thank You for the people You've given me to love, heavenly Father. Be with me as I plan to show Your love through a welcoming spirit and hospitality this week.

DIVINE APPOINTMENTS

8

Paul and his companions traveled throughout the region of Phrygia and Galatia, having been kept by the Holy Spirit from preaching the word in the province of Asia.

ACTS 16:6 NIV

I can't believe it. I have to switch schools. And I didn't even move. I live in the same house I've always lived in. Our town has been growing so fast that a new high school was built. I'll admit, the high school I've been at for three years (yes, three years!) was overcrowded. I took half my classes in trailers they set up outside the regular building. But a new school for my senior year? No way. Doesn't seem fair. The worse part is, our baseball team is getting torn in half. This was supposed to be our year to compete for the conference championship. Now there's no way. My parents tell me that I need to go with the flow. But all I feel is disappointed! And mad!

—Hunter, age 18

Where does God want you to be? The easy answer is, right where you are.

But what about when things change? What about when we end up where we didn't expect or maybe even want to be? Does that mean God made a mistake? Does that mean something needs to get fixed, pronto?

Not so fast. If you want to know where God wants you to serve Him, simply ask Him to show you and then keep your eyes open to the opportunities all around you. Did you know there are ways you can make a difference in the world that might come as a complete surprise to you—but never to God?

God loves to create "divine appointments," where He brings people into our lives at just the right moment and, likewise, puts us in the paths of others when they need to hear a word of wisdom or encouragement from us.

When your well-laid-out plans suddenly get changed, instead of grumbling and getting frustrated, instead of assuming that a thing is terribly wrong, consider the possibility that God is up to something.

Paul had plans to minister in a town called Bithynia. Once Paul knew what was next on his agenda he was always full steam ahead. But God had plans for him to minister in Macedonia and introduce the Good News to a whole new continent (see Acts 16:6–10). He was led by the Spirit in a dream and told to change his plans immediately. He did and embarked upon a period of remarkable ministry.

As you make plans for your upcoming year and beyond, keep your heart and eyes open. Who knows what is next for you? The same Spirit of God that led Paul will lead you too.

TRAINING TIP

A steady routine can be great. But sometimes change is even better. Switch up your workouts a little. If you've been doing bench presses, switch to some push-ups and shoulder presses. In other words, keep your body guessing so it gets the full benefit of your exercise.

GAME PLAN

In sports, one key to success is to be ready for anything. If you're expecting a curveball, you might get tricked with a fastball. If you're expecting a spike, a soft tip can leave you on the ground wondering what happened. Make a plan, but be ready for anything.

What are five things you hope to make happen in the next year of your life? Write them down. Plans and goals are great. But then say a prayer where you let God know that you are open to whatever He wants to accomplish in your life.

PRAYER

God, Thank You for Your Spirit to guide and direct my steps.

8

TAKE A BREAK

Those who live in the shelter
of the Most High will find rest
in the shadow of the Almighty.
PSALM 91:1 NLT

I'm worried about my friend Ella. Don't get me wrong; she is Superwoman. She does everything incredibly well. She gets straight A's. She leads Bible study in our sports huddle. She is a superstar volleyball player. She volunteers as a tutor. I asked her how much sleep she gets, and she told me it's less than six hours a night. She is the most disciplined and committed person I know. But lately she has been getting sick a lot. Is it possible she is pushing too hard? Count me as a worried friend.

—Chelsea, age 16

According to Genesis 2:2–3, even God rested after creating the universe: "On the seventh day God had finished his work of creation, so he rested from all his work. And God blessed the seventh day and declared it holy, because it was the day when he rested from all his work of creation" (NLT).

God needed a break? He may not have needed a break, but He declared a holy day of rest. Unlike God, we get tired. When our bodies and brains are tired, they don't function like they were created to do. We need the renewal that comes from rest. But just as much as we need physical rest, we need to recharge our spirits too. We need to take a moment at the end of the day to simply take a deep breath and say a short prayer of praise and thanksgiving to take care of our souls.

Few men lived as intense a life as King David. He was a kingdom builder, dealing with the high demand of politics. He was a creative poet and songwriter, pouring his heart into writing and collecting psalms. He was a general and a warrior, tested on the field of battle with strategic and physical challenges. He faced strife and danger—some of it self-induced—his entire adult life. He was an emotional man who was subject to the same laws of fatigue and exhaustion as the rest of us. Is it any wonder he described the blessed man as one who meditates on God in the morning and at night (Psalm 1:2)? Is it any wonder that he found rest in the shadow of the Almighty (Psalm 91:1)?

Sometimes we run the risk of burning ourselves out even in doing good things. Sleep deprivation is a major danger in our modern society. If you are pushing yourself hard in sports, this makes rest and sleep even more important!

Don't wait until the point of exhaustion to take time to slow down; thank God for His love and support, and ask Him for His help and grace.

Jesus knows we must come apart and rest awhile, or else we may just plain come apart.

TRAINING TIP

To be the best athlete possible, your body needs great nutrition, great workouts, and great rest. Jesus reminds us that God created the Sabbath (a day of rest) for our own benefit, both spiritually and physically. (See Mark 2:27 below.)

GAME PLAN

Then Jesus said to them, "The Sabbath was made to meet the needs of people, and not people to meet the requirements of the Sabbath" (NLT). Use that verse to evaluate whether you are experiencing a Sabbath rest in your life.

- Do you get enough sleep?
- Do you have quiet time with just you and God?
- Do you know when your body needs a break?

PRAYER

Dear Lord, I need Your refreshing, renewing grace to keep me going. Thank You for Your gift of rest!

OBEDIENT STRENGTH

Sovereign Lord, remember me. Please, God, strengthen me just once more, and let me with one blow get revenge on the Philistines for my two eyes.
JUDGES 16:28 NIV

My high school wrestling team is ranked #1 in the state. We have a great coach, and our team is great every year. It is an honor to be on the team and even more of an honor to be a starter. It's my senior year. I've been grinding hard all year to be on the mat for my team every match. The good news is, I just got named to start at the 120-pound weight class. The bad news is that it is tough for me to make weigh-in at 120. My best weight is right around 125 pounds. Lower than that, I don't feel as strong. However, our 126-pound wrestler is the best in the state in that class. I can't beat him. And I can't move up and beat the 132-pounder either. I can safely keep five pounds off before every meet. I'm just praying that I can keep my strength!

—Wyatt, age 18

If you wanted to play football, or if you suspected that a group of tough guys were going to jump you, you definitely wanted Samson on your side. When teams were picked, his name would have always been called first. His name is synonymous with strength and power.

As a youth, he killed a lion. When ambushed by a small squadron of Philistines, he dispatched thirty men without breaking a sweat. Even when he became entangled with Delilah, he continued to be victorious on brute strength. Tied up to be captured, Samson escaped by breaking free from coils of ropes and cutting through one thousand men who were waiting to enslave him.

Samson's mother committed him to the Lord when he was a baby. He took the vows of a Nazirite, which meant no fermented beverages and no cutting his hair. The cousin of Jesus, John the Baptist, took the same vows.

It was only when Samson rejected his vows before God, allowing his hair to be cut, that the Philistines could subdue him, again relying on the charms of Delilah to set the trap. He was chained to a millstone. His eyes were poked out. He was flogged. As a final humiliation, the rulers of the Philistines brought him to the temple to be mocked. God answered Samson's prayer and, in a single moment, he accomplished more than he had at any other time in his life. He pushed down the pillars of the Philistine temple and destroyed three thousand men.

Despite his disobedience, God used Samson when he repented. But is it possible God would have done even greater things had Samson always been obedient?

TRAINING TIP

There are a lot of legal and illegal supplements that promise to make you stronger. Some of them work at building muscle, but some are very bad for your overall health. Never take a supplement that is illegal. Be sure you consult with your coach, parents, trainer, and doctor before taking legal supplements to enhance your athletic performance.

GAME PLAN

Samson was born with a supernatural strength. It was a gift from God to be used for God. As a baby, Samson's parents committed him to God for service. Samson lost his divine gift through disobedience. He regained his divine gift through renewed obedience.

What is a gift God has given you? How can you use this gift to serve God and others? Are you committed to a life of obedience?

PRAYER

Heavenly Father, forgive any sin in my life and help me to trust and obey You each day. Grant me the strength of spirit and character that come through obedience.

PUT ON THE ARMOR

But since we belong to the day,
let us be sober, putting on faith
and love as a breastplate, and
the hope of salvation as a helmet.
I THESSALONIANS 5:8 NIV

It's hard to say whether my family is middle class or maybe poor. I know there's a lot of things my friends have that I don't have. But I'm not complaining. I get along great with my parents and I don't feel like I'm missing out on anything. That's why it came as such a shock when my dad came home from work and handed me a shoebox. He told me to go ahead and open it up. I did and found a pair of running shoes that cost a ton of money. I couldn't believe it. No way could he afford to spend that kind of money on something like track. What I had been wearing was fine. When I protested, he just smiled and said, "As hard as you're working, I wanted you to have the best equipment possible. Consider it an early birthday gift." The amount of respect my dad showed for me was the best gift of all.

—Kennedy, age 13

You can't play soccer without shin guards. You can't play football without a helmet. You can't play softball or baseball without a glove. You can't box without a mouth guard, gloves, and headgear.

None of us would go to battle as a soldier without the proper weapons. It would be a foolish act of suicide. Soldiers need offensive and defensive weapons. In the battle for our soul, we need weapons, too!

God sees us in our need, saves us from our sins, and puts us on the right path to live for Him. Our life changes for the better. We are thankful. But sometimes we get proud or complacent. We begin to feel that we have everything under control and grow self-sufficient. We forget that God is the One who turned our lives around in the first place. We make a mess of things. But God sees us, hears our call for help, redeems us, and puts us on solid ground again. And oftentimes, again and again.

Rather than live in a cycle of defeat, wouldn't it be better to remember—to never forget—that God is the Source of our salvation and strength? In Ephesians 6:11 and following, Paul tells us to put on the whole armor of God, including the sword of truth, the breastplate of righteousness, and the shield of faith. None of those defenses come from our strength and savvy but are gifts from God to claim and cling onto.

Are you trying to master your life with your own sufficiency and strength? Are you trying to fight spiritual battles without a sword, a breastplate, or a shield? Or are you wearing His armor?

TRAINING TIP

Sports equipment can be very expensive. You already knew that! You don't have to buy the most expensive to have good quality shoes and other equipment. If you can't afford shoes and gear that will keep you safe and healthy, make sure you check online at sites that sell discontinued models that are still perfectly fine. Also there are secondhand sports shops that might have just what you need for a fraction of the cost.

GAME PLAN

Satan attacks us as a "roaring lion" or, more often, as an "angel of light." When he comes as an angel, it is so he can sneak up on us when our defenses are down. Most of all, it is so he looks attractive and can trick us through his lies. He is the "father of lies," after all.

What are some lies that Satan has tried to spread to you? To your friends? In our society? How can we protect ourselves from his lies?

PRAYER

Lord, I acknowledge my need for You. You are my strength and salvation. Help me to walk humbly with You. Don't let me fall prey to the attacks of Satan.

THE RIGHT PLACE AT THE RIGHT TIME

For if you remain silent at this time, relief and deliverance for the Jews will arise from another place, but you and your father's family will perish. And who knows but that you have come to your royal position for such a time as this?

ESTHER 4:14 NIV

I'm kind of bummed out. I'm not getting along with a group of girls on my lacrosse team. But I did what I thought I had to do. A couple of them were teasing Abby all the time. Abby's a little heavy, but who cares? We've all got something we struggle with. Plus, she's a great athlete. They were constantly putting her down and calling her some bad names I won't even say out loud. I didn't pay attention for a while, but I finally had enough. I did some yelling back at them for being so cruel. Now they are calling me names and trying to give me a tough time. I can handle it because I know I did the right thing. I just don't understand how people can be so mean to others.

—Brittany, age 13

Esther was a beautiful young Jewish woman living in Persia who was raised by her cousin Mordecai as a daughter. Esther was taken to the house of Xerxes, king of Persia, to become one of his many wives. Her beauty and character were remarkable, and Xerxes appointed her as his queen. He did not know that Esther was a Jew, because Mordecai, perhaps sensing danger, had told her not to reveal her identity.

Haman, an advisor to the king, hated Mordecai because Mordecai refused to bow down to him, so he hatched a plot of revenge. Haman went to Xerxes and told him the Jewish people were disobedient and could not be trusted (3:8). Xerxes told Haman to do whatever he thought best. The evil man planned to exterminate every Jew living in the city of Sousa.

Mordecai appealed Esther to speak to the king on behalf of her people. This was a dangerous assignment because anyone who came into the king's presence without being summoned could be put to death. Esther had recently witnessed the previous queen's execution for displeasing the king. Esther fasted for three days, then went to the king. He welcomed her. She told Xerxes of Haman's plans against her people. Her faith won the king's favor, saving the Jews. Haman and his ten sons were hanged on the gallows that had been built for Mordecai.

God's deliverance does not always show up in the form of a miracle. In this case, His providence put Esther in the right place at the right time. Deliverance came through the courageous faithfulness of His servant.

Has God put you in a particular place to make a difference?

TRAINING TIP

Bad training habits lead to bad performances when the games start. Bad spiritual habits lead to bad spiritual performance when temptation or hard times come your way.

GAME PLAN

Being in the right place at the right time sounds exciting. But sometimes it is the hardest place to be!

Has there been a time when you have needed to stand up and say or do the right thing even though it was tough? How can you prepare yourself to be ready when that moment comes for you?

PRAYER

Dear God, give me the courage to stand up for what is right. Thank You for putting me in the right place at the right time.

ROLL UP YOUR SLEEVES

So roll up your sleeves, put your mind in gear, be totally ready to receive the gift that's coming when Jesus arrives. Don't lazily slip back into those old grooves of evil, doing just what you feel like doing. You didn't know any better then; you do now.
I PETER 1:13-14 THE MESSAGE

I can't believe it. I just got benched. I've been the starting power forward for my high school basketball team. It hurt when my name wasn't called as the announcer introduced the starting lineups. I think I turned a little red from embarrassment. But what hurts most is what my coach said to me. He said, "Jacob, you're still a good player. But you haven't put in the work this off-season. I assumed you'd be my starter again this year, but you haven't earned it." I'm mad. But not at Coach. I'm mad at myself, because he's right. I think this is a wake-up call in a bunch of areas of my life. I've gotten lazy, and it's time I get moving.

—Jacob, age 17

Peter warns against laziness and how detrimental it is to our spiritual vitality and strength. He wants us to roll up our sleeves—not to earn or preserve our salvation, but as an expression of gratitude as we draw closer to God. A verse later Peter describes God's response to whether we are diligent or lazy this way: "You call out to God for help and he helps—he's a good Father that way. But don't forget, he's also a responsible Father, and won't let you get by with sloppy living" (I Peter 1:17 The Message).

"Idleness is the devil's workshop" is not a quote from the Bible, but it has its roots in scripture. Solomon says: "One who is slack in his work is brother to one who destroys" (Proverbs 18:9 NIV). Being a slacker is harmful to us and others. Paul says: "We hear that some among you are idle and disruptive. They are not busy; they are busybodies" (II Thessalonians 3:11 NIV). By not using their time productively, these people were inappropriately meddling in the lives of others who were busy. Paul goes even further about the danger of idleness in another letter: "They get into the habit of being idle and going about from house to house. And not only do they become idlers, but also busybodies who talk nonsense, saying things they ought not to" (I Timothy 5:13 NIV).

Idleness is not the same as rest. The Bible commands us to rest (the Sabbath), and taking breaks from work is good. Being lazy means we are doing nothing when we should be doing something.

We live in a sinful world. A person who doesn't have something purposeful to do will invariably be more tempted to fall into sin. Satan is very eager to supply us with bad things to do when we are idle.

Do you need to roll up your sleeves, beginning today?

TRAINING TIP

How do you get in a good workout or practice hard when you are feeling particularly lazy?

- **Get started.** Once you get moving, laziness has a way of disappearing.
- **Reward yourself.** Bribing yourself won't always work. It's better to go hard because you want to. But every now and then you need to promise yourself a treat for going hard when you don't feel like it.
- **Get help.** If it's off-season and you aren't working out with the team, it's very easy to take a day off. Have a workout partner to hold you accountable.

GAME PLAN

Have you let yourself slide in your spiritual walk with God? Don't give up! In James 4:8 we read: "Come close to God, and God will come close to you" (NLT). How can you draw close to God today?

Get away from distractions, including your smartphone. Take a 30-minute walk just to pray. Tell God what is in your heart and listen to His still, small voice for guidance.

PRAYER

Thank You, heavenly Father, that You are the God of love and mercy. Thank You also that You expect my best—and that You provide the strength and grace I need to please You with my work and life.

START EARLY

Listen to my voice in the morning, LORD.
Each morning I bring my requests
to you and wait expectantly.

PSALM 5:3 NLT

I mean to have devotions every day. But by the time I run out the door to get to school, go to basketball practice or a game after school, do my homework, and maybe watch one TV show, I am too tired. I open my Bible and fall asleep before I even say a prayer. How can I get into the habit of quiet time with God every day?

—Shandra, age 14

STUDY VERSES: Psalm 143:1–8

As an athlete, do you wake up a few minutes before an important game, throw on your uniform, stumble to the car, sleep on the drive over, and suddenly wake up in the parking lot minutes before your meet or match is about to begin? Is that the best plan to secure a victory?

Most great athletes would answer, "No. You gotta get started early if you are going to be ready to compete at your best." Watching swimmers and runners and other great athletes in the Olympics, I was reminded of their commitment to train hard and a lifestyle of constant preparation. Some of their warm-ups would be more than a workout for many of us!

Throughout Psalm 143, David is in a fight for his life. His enemies have him surrounded. His faith is starting to waver. He's not sure God is there to help him. What does he remember to do? "Let me hear of your unfailing love each morning, for I am trusting you. Show me where to walk, for I give myself to you" (v. 8 NLT). He turns to God in the morning. He starts his day by asking for God's guidance.

How about our spiritual lives? Do we share this same commitment to preparation? What comes first each day? How do we start our morning? Do we prepare ourselves spiritually to face the daily challenges and battles of life?

To be aware of God's favor and presence in your every moment of the day is one of the greatest treasures you'll ever discover. That discovery happens when you "look up" in the morning and throughout the day, getting your attitude and expectations attuned to hearing God's voice.

Prepare for life every morning. Open your eyes, take a breath, and then thank God for the new day. Look to heaven and ask God for wisdom, direction, and courage, that your life would be a blessing to everyone you encounter.

TRAINING TIP

It is essential for athletes to provide their body with the fuel needed to compete. The most-skipped meal is the most important meal for making sure your body has the energy it needs. Maybe you're not a morning person. How can you help yourself get out of bed a little earlier every day to provide nourishment for body and soul?

GAME PLAN

Don't be a chicken. Just do it. Even if it means going to bed a little earlier, be courageous.

Reach out your hand and set your alarm for thirty minutes earlier to give yourself time to be alone with God!

PRAYER

In the morning I will look up to You for guidance and strength, to express my love and gratitude to You, my Lord.

MADE NEW

But those who hope in the Lᴏʀᴅ will renew their strength. They will soar on wings like eagles; they will run and not grow weary, they will walk and not be faint.

ISAIAH 40:31

To be honest, I don't feel very close to God. I've gotten myself into some bad stuff. I'm not even going to say what it is. My attitudes aren't positive. I'm mad all the time. It seems like I fight with my parents and even my friends constantly. I don't know what's happened in my life. I used to be considered the "good kid." Not anymore. To make matters worse, I'm supposed to meet with my coach this afternoon. I think he might be ready to kick me off the team. I did something pretty stupid last week and got a one-day in-school suspension. I'm in a lot of trouble everywhere. I don't know how to get my life straightened out.

—Kenny, age 15

STUDY VERSES: Psalm 51:12

In a world that can wear us down mentally, physically, and spiritually, how do we renew our strength? What do we do in the face of too many projects, too many temptations, too many conflicts, and too many other soul- and energy-sapping dynamics at work in life?

The prophet Isaiah ministered to a nation on the verge of collapse. It wasn't just the acute threat from foreign powers—though that was an obvious stressor—but the once-proud and -righteous country was sinking in a mire created by its own cynicism and corruption. His antidote to spiritual fatigue was simple: hope in the Lord.

David went through a horrible period in his life that included the worst sin of all: murder. Throughout Psalm 51, he turns to God with absolute humility and sorrow. He knows how bad he has been. He seeks a renewed life, a new life, through the forgiveness that only God can provide.

Others might help you in times of trouble. Great. But don't put your hope in them. You might be able to muster some more determination to get moving in the right direction spiritually. Wonderful. But don't even place your hope in yourself. The only place to turn for a renewed spirit is to the One who has given you every good and perfect gift, including any strength or talent you were born with. What a wonderful promise, that we can run without growing weary!

So how is your day? How has your week been going? How does this month look to be shaping up for you? Are you hopeful and inspired? Or are you discouraged? Either way, place your hope in the Lord and let Him renew your strength so that you can run and not grow weary.

TRAINING TIP

Saint Augustine put it so clearly when he said: "When God is our strength, it is strength indeed; when our strength is our own, it is only weakness."

GAME PLAN

The Psalms are the "prayer book" of the Bible. Most were written or collected by King David, a mighty warrior with a tender heart. He had many flaws, but he had a heart to love and serve God.

Write your own psalm today. Write down a prayer for spiritual renewal. Keep it somewhere convenient where you can refer to it often when your faith seems weak.

PRAYER

Heavenly Father, You truly are the Source of my hope for today, tomorrow, and all the days ahead of me. Thank You.

FIRST THINGS FIRST

Seek the Kingdom of God above all else,
and live righteously, and he will give you
everything you need.
MATTHEW 6:33 NLT

An exchange student from South American lived with my family this past school year. It worked out perfectly for Gonzalo to play on my school's soccer team with me. He was unbelievable. We were an okay team. With him, we were a great team. We made it all the way to the quarterfinals of the state tournament. We were talking in the back row of my dad's SUV when my family was driving him to the airport to return to Argentina. I asked him what his favorite thing was while living with us. He mentioned a number of things. But I was surprised when he didn't say "soccer." I asked him why. His answer was, "I love everything about being here. You're my friend forever. I love football, too. But you and many of your friends are too crazy for sports." That got me wondering. Is it possible to let sports be too important?

—Von, age 17

STUDY VERSES: Matthew 6:19–34

What is most important to you? Have you put God first in your life?

Sports are great. But the most important thing in your life is not how good you are at—

Volleyball
Baseball
Football
Basketball
Gymnastics
Skateboarding
Tennis
Lacrosse
Cheerleading
Wrestling
Or ANY OTHER SPORT you play!

School is important. Getting good grades is important. But that's not what is most important in your life.

Friendship is also very important. But being popular and getting along with others is not what is most important for you.

What matters most? Knowing how much God loves you and loving Him with all your heart, mind, and strength. That's when every other area of your life falls into place.

When Jesus was asked what mattered most (by someone who was actually more interested in putting Jesus down), we read: "Teacher, which is the most important commandment in the law of Moses?" Jesus replied, " 'You must love the LORD your God with all your heart, all your soul, and all your mind.' This is the first and greatest commandment.

A second is equally important: 'Love your neighbor as yourself.' The entire law and all the demands of the prophets are based on these two commandments" (Matthew 22:36–40 NLT).

TRAINING TIP

Your parents love you. Your teachers and coaches want the very best for you. But here is the best news of all. God knows you best and loves you most.

GAME PLAN

How do you make God first in your life? It takes the same enthusiasm and discipline you put into your sports.

Read the Bible, His Word. Pray often. Go to church and get involved with other Christians. Most of all, fall in love with God again every single day.

PRAYER

Heavenly Father, help me to always keep You as the center of my life. Help me to never let anything be more important to me than being loved by You and loving You.

PROMISES FOR ATHLETES

HE IS WITH YOU

Haven't I commanded you? Strength! Courage! Don't be timid; don't get discouraged. God, your God, is with you every step you take. JOSHUA 1:9 THE MESSAGE

HE PROTECTS YOU

Love the Lord, all you godly ones! For the Lord protects those who are loyal to him, but he harshly punishes the arrogant. So be strong and courageous, all you who put your hope in the Lord! PSALM 31:23-24 NLT

HE RENEWS YOU

But those who trust in the Lord will find new strength. They will soar high on wings like eagles. They will run and not grow weary. They will walk and not faint. ISAIAH 40:31 NLT

HE HAS A WONDERFUL PLAN FOR YOU LIFE

Meanwhile, the moment we get tired in the waiting, God's Spirit is right alongside helping us along. If we don't know how or what to pray, it doesn't matter. He does our praying in and for us, making prayer out of our wordless sighs, our aching groans. He knows us far better than we know ourselves, knows our pregnant condition, and keeps us present before God. That's why we can be so sure that every detail in our lives of love for God is worked into something good. ROMANS 8:26-28 THE MESSAGE

HE WILL NEVER ABANDON YOU

For God has said, "I will never fail you. I will never abandon you." So we can say with confidence, "The LORD is my helper, so I will have no fear. What can mere people do to me?" HEBREWS 13:5-6 NLT

HE GUIDES AND DIRECTS YOU

Trust in the LORD with all your heart and lean not on your own understanding; in all your ways submit to him, and he will make your paths straight. PROVERBS 3:5-6 NIV

The LORD directs the steps of the godly. He delights in every detail of their lives. PSALM 37:23 NLT

A man's heart plans his way, but the LORD directs his steps. PROVERBS 16:9 NKJV

HE HEARS YOUR PRAYERS

Call to me and I will answer you, and will tell you great and hidden things that you have not known. JEREMIAH 33:3 ESV

HE GIVES YOU TRUE JOY

"I have loved you even as the Father has loved me. Remain in my love. When you obey my commandments, you remain in my love, just as I obey my Father's commandments and remain in his love. I have told you these things so that you will be filled with my joy. Yes, your joy will overflow!" JOHN 15:9-11 NLT

HE GIVES YOU ETERNAL LIFE

Do not love the world or the things in the world. If anyone loves the world, the love of the Father is not in him. For all that is in the world—the lust of the flesh, the lust of the eyes, and the pride of life—is not of the Father but is of the world. And the world is passing away, and the lust of it; but he who does the will of God abides forever. I JOHN 2:15-17 NKJV

HE FORGIVES YOU

If we confess our sins, he is faithful and just to forgive us our sins and to cleanse us from all unrighteousness. I JOHN 1:9 ESV

HE GIVES YOU PEACE

Do not worry about anything, but pray and ask God for everything you need, always giving thanks. And God's peace, which is so great we cannot understand it, will keep your hearts and minds in Christ Jesus. PHILIPPIANS 4:6-7 NCV

"I am leaving you with a gift—peace of mind and heart. And the peace I give is a gift the world cannot give. So don't be troubled or afraid." JOHN 14:27 NLT

HE GIVES YOU WISDOM

If you need wisdom, ask our generous God, and he will give it to you. He will not rebuke you for asking. JAMES 1:5 NLT

For the LORD gives wisdom; from his mouth come knowledge and understanding. He holds success in store for the upright, he is a shield to those whose walk is blameless. PROVERBS 2:6-7 NIV

ABOUT THE AUTHOR

Mark Gilroy is the father of six children and coached them in several sports for 26 seasons. Mark loves sports and kids and believes there are many life skills and lessons that are developed by participating in athletics. He is a longtime publishing executive and has written six best-selling novels. He and his wife, Amy, reside in Brentwood, Tennessee.

DaySpring
LIVE YOUR FAITH

Dear Friend,

This book was prayerfully crafted with you, the reader, in mind—every word, every sentence, every page—was thoughtfully written, designed, and packaged to encourage you...right where you are this very moment. At DaySpring, our vision is to see every person experience the life-changing message of God's love. So, as we worked through rough drafts, design changes, edits, and details, we prayed for you to deeply experience His unfailing love, indescribable peace, and pure joy. It is our sincere hope that through these Truth-filled pages your heart will be blessed, knowing that God cares about you—your desires and disappointments, your challenges and dreams.

He knows. He cares. He loves you unconditionally.

BLESSINGS!
THE DAYSPRING BOOK TEAM